I0201540

OEDIPUS MAX

An American Family

A memoir by

David and Sid Bennett

OEDIPUS MAX

First Edition, 2015

Library of Congress Control Number 2015904819

ISBN Number 978-0-9822663-1-1

Copyright Sid Bennett 2015

All rights reserved. No part of this book may be reproduced in any form or by any means without the written permission of the Publisher, excepting brief quotes in connection with reviews written specifically for inclusion in a magazine or newspaper.

Photographs are from Bennett family collections.

Published by

Frog Pond Studio
P.O. Box 1323
Harwich, MA 02645
508 430 0264

Table of Contents

FOREWORD: David

One night on Cape Cod, I was having dinner with my friends Keith and Margaret Casey Gould at their getaway house in Chatham.

Keith is a retired creative director from the advertising business, but is still active with free-lance and writing movie scripts with a TV commercials director he had worked with a lot.

Margaret was the famous "Casey" who was secretary to David McCall of McCaffery & McCall, where we had all met.

I told them some funny story about Max, and also one of the serious ones, a family legend that when he had come over to America at the age of 14, that he had to go back because of bad papers or something, but I wasn't sure if it was true, or if I had made it up in my head. Certainly I had never asked Max and there wasn't anyone around to ask anymore.

The Gould's knew I was working on a book about radio shock-jocks.

Keith said, "Why are you writing about those jerks? You should be writing about your father."

I took it negatively. I thought that attacking the shock-jocks was important. "Hey, don't tell me what to write about." I wasn't even sure if we were kidding or not.

Keith got up from the table and paced into the living room and back into the dining room, going on with his theme, saying, "I wish I had a family as interesting as that to write about." Margaret said, "Anyone can write a book about shock-jocks. Only you can write a book about your father."

I went home sobered by their talk, and wrote down a list of 32 anecdotes connected to Max. I began to get excited. The Goulds were right. Certainly I had enough quantitatively. If I could bring some quality to it, it could be a great project.

*****

Something we all have in common is that we don't ask our parents and relatives enough questions while they are alive, and then when they are gone, we think of hundreds of questions we wished we had asked. This is being modified in the Millennium, which is becoming The Age of the Memoir, probably led by Tom Brokaw's book, "The Greatest Generation", which has apparently precipitated the questioning, by their children, for the first time, of World War II veterans who never told them much about their experiences.

I am a prize example of the non-questioning offspring. Though I knew a lot about my father from day-to-day dealings with him, I never asked details, especially about his childhood. My two brothers and my sister and I had a tiny smattering of anecdotes about his life before he came to America, but nothing significant.

Now that I urgently began writing about this colorful immigrant, I realized how little I knew about him.

A long period of fun and agonizing work started. I was spending five and ten hours a week on the phone with my brother Sid, discussing and arguing. We had sharply differing opinions of some of our mutual memories. I was also calling and corresponding with a small number of relatives and friends.

Then one day when I was spending a few days on Cape Cod, my brother, who is retired on the Cape, called me and said, "You better get over here, I think I found a gold mine."

The "gold mine" turned out to be a small beat-up blue suitcase. Inside was a lot of Max paraphernalia, including letters, documents, and most importantly, two "diaries." One was on loose letter-size sheets, and one was on a 3X5 white pad gummed at the top. Max was about 80 when he wrote these. Apparently he was not waiting to be asked questions.

Max taught himself to read and write English and the handwriting is scrawly and hard to read. But of course it is more than worth the effort.

These diaries fired me up all over again about the book and radically altered my approach.

*****

I hero-worshipped Joe, my older brother, and I hero-worshipped Eddie Walsh, who taught me meat cutting in my father's store, but I never hero-worshipped my father, Max Bennett.

He was a little bigger than life, surprising you one minute with his strength, the next with how smart he was, the next with how serious he could be, and the next how funny.

We had only a handful of real conversations, I realize many years later, but he had a tremendous influence on me.

He and my mother Lillian were masters of an instinctive silence-with-no-punishment when we did something wrong, which is a powerful way to build a thinking brain and a conscience in a child, and I recommend it to all the psychologists who want everybody to "talk it out" all the time.

I never thought of writing anything about him, and when I did, I was hit hard by how little I knew about him. We were a classic of the American family who never asked enough questions, or hardly any questions at all.

I knew that this dramatic immigrant had come to the United States alone at the age of 14 and some sketchy information about his life in Lithuania. What I knew most was the years when everything revolved around the Norwood Market, the meat and fish store that Max owned. We all worked there, starting at age 13 or so. And we all had to deal with this operatic character.

*****

Where you grew up is an accident of your family's history.

For me, it was Everett, Massachusetts, and a lifetime later I found out it was because my father bought a store there when he was young and just married.

He didn't pick Everett. He picked the store, and it could have been in any suburb of Boston, like Malden or Medford or Somerville.

Lucky for him, and lucky for me.

*****

Anyone familiar with Jewish culture will recognize this as a Kaddish for Max. I realized it about halfway through the writing. A Kaddish is the Hebrew prayer for the dead.

So it is a Kaddish. I have tremendous respect and gratitude for him. He did the best he knew how, all through his life.

And he gave me America.

FOREWORD: Sid

David and I had talked about my participation in the book, but I felt it would be minimal. When I questioned the title, he just said I didn't understand enough of the modern view of the Oedipus Complex.

During David's memorial celebration in June 2005, in his son Michael's eulogy he mentioned that David was writing a book about Max. Then he coolly said to everybody, "Now Sid has to finish it".

I cringed. David and I had some things in common. First, we were world-class procrastinators. Then, even if we started something, it became very difficult to completely finish anything.

During a visit to David in New York soon after he graduated The University of Missouri, he told me that two of his classmates had already published books. I asked him how come he hadn't written a book. Are they better than he is? He said, "The only difference between them and me is that they sat down at a typewriter and did it. I haven't done that." It was immediately clear that he and I had the same problem. For instance, I didn't apply to colleges until too late in my senior year of high school.

Thanks to Michael, a box of David's stories and notes plus the Blue Suitcase came to me soon after the celebration.

In the winter of 2014 I was in the middle of one of my unfinished projects, - namely, clearing out my cellar - when I saw the box with DAVID written on it. I looked inside. There was a notebook that contained class notes on how to make a film. There were loose papers. And there was a large three-hole notebook with Mickey Mouse on the cover. His use of Mickey Mouse was not surprising. He had a Mickey Mouse wrist watch at one point.

Inside the notebook were stories stapled separately and more loose papers - all were part of *Oedipus Max*.

I hadn't planned on spending a lot of time in my cellar that day. Cellars on Cape Cod in January can be very cold. Do I continue to clear up or do I go to my nice warm desk to look this stuff over and maybe start to edit a book? Why not? I already had one unfinished book in my desk because I couldn't get the ending correct. I may as well try another. I made a quick decision and carried the notebook upstairs.

I surprised myself - I sorted papers, made PDF's, converted same to Word, had infinite problems with various fonts and hidden formatting, had my granddaughter Lily finally do a clean type of David's writing so that I could get on with it - and finish it?

What follows is a result of that decision.

ACKNOWLEDGEMENTS

David's son Michael saved many of Max's notes from a cellar flood. His daughter Kate saved David's CD's and notes. His daughter Laurie saved David from becoming a world-class grouch.

Sid owes any computer, electronic, or smart phone knowledge that he has to his son Stephen. He owes some excellent suggestions to his daughter Leslie. He owes many happy local hours away from his desk to his son Peter. He owes the prodding of his son Roger for acquiring knowledge of the distant world and his genealogy. He owes his present condition to his late wife Betsy. If it weren't for her, he would weigh 350 pounds, be dead, or be a miserable person.

Sid's granddaughter Lily deserves a special prize for the most practical contribution by typing hundreds of pages of manuscript and Sid's daughter-in-law Gisele deserves a prize for the hours she spent creating and correcting the PDF.

ONE NIGHT IN A TRIPLE DECKER: David

In 1934, when I was eight, we lived in the middle floor of a triple-decker on Vine Street in Everett, and the kitchen table, where we ate most of our meals, was next to twin windows.

It was September, and there was plenty of light coming through at suppertime. The evening meal scene was repeated a couple of hundred times during the year with slight variations, but tonight would be different enough to remember forever.

My father, Max Bennett, owned a meat and fish store in downtown Everett, a twenty-minute walk from the house. The store closed at 6pm and he always came right home to preside over supper at the kitchen table.

He was the most interesting person I ever knew, a handsome, successful man with some quirks and contradictions. For instance, he was famous for eating only once a day, so these meals were serious.

My mother Lillian dished up lots of food, like a platter piled high with rib lamb chops or a platter of haddock fillets.

My mother dipped fish in egg and breadcrumbs and fried the haddock in Crisco in cast-iron pans. Steaks and chops were "pan-broiled", which meant fried with no fat added to the pan. There were boiled potatoes and vegetables like string beans, and some rye bread or challah. "Salad" was chunks of iceberg lettuce and tomatoes, with Cain's mayonnaise on the side.

We all ate soup first, but Max would not change from some old habit of eating soup last, and Lillian dished it up dutifully. She was cheerful about this as she also followed American customs and tried to keep a Kosher home at the same time.

Like other New Englanders, we had frankfurters and beans on Saturday nights, and salmon and peas on the Fourth of July, but Max and the soup became a symbol of his stubbornness, and the way he could dig in his heels without regard for the opinion of others. But he was a self-made man, and wasn't used to questioning himself.

On this particular night, the whole family was at supper, not a common event. My four year-old kid brother Sidney, my 13 year-old sister Sylvia, and my 16 year-old brother Joey, my mother, and me.

Syl wasn't always there, because there were lots of evenings when she was "gallivanting around" with her girlfriends.

Joey, already in college, was often missing because he was studying somewhere. We watched Max's every move, because it was fun.

First there was the removal of the suit jacket and tie, and the rolling up of the sleeves, washing his hands, and then sitting at the head of the table like a football tackle at a training camp meal.

Then the belt of Canadian Club - about two to six ounces in a water tumbler, downed in one or two swallows.

I usually sat at the foot of the table and there was a small radio on a chest behind me. Starting at 6:30, Lowell Thomas delivered the news in his stentorian tones. Then at 7pm, Amos and Andy, who made everyone laugh. Inevitably, we would start chattering and laughing and Max would issue a loud "Shaaa!" and we would subside for a while. The house would get quiet after that. Max usually went to bed very early, tired from his long day, and a little sedated by the Canadian Club. He might look at the Sunday New York Times, which he read through the week, but not for very long each day.

Sometimes he was in bed before Sidney.

It seems as if everyone always said, in trying to describe my father, that he was "built like a bull." He was about five-feet-nine and big in the shoulders and chest. He had a big dramatic head like Spencer Tracy, and in fact, looked like the actor. He had a startlingly white complexion and rosy red circles about the size of half-dollars on his cheeks. At 42, his hair was black with some gray, full and wavy. He was the absolutely reliable, deep-rock foundation of my life and of the rest of the family. From my first awareness at age three or four, and for decades, I knew he was leaving the house about 4:30am five days a week, heading for Boston's Faneuil Hall wholesale market to buy meat, and to the Boston Harbor piers to buy fish for the Norwood Market, which was the center of all our lives. I only saw him leave the house a couple times a year, but that's all you need to get a great feeling of security you couldn't possibly articulate at that age.

At eight, I was enjoying everything, drifting along through all this happily. I loved school; I loved hanging out at the store. I even liked Hebrew School four afternoons a week and Sunday midday. And I loved being with the family. My mother, under five feet and gradually being overtaken in height by all four of her children, with a sense of humor, piercing intelligent eyes, and silky hair so black it looked blue sometimes.

Joey, 16 and automatically a hero of mine because he was nine years older than me, but also because a crowd of teenage hulks called for him every morning to escort him to high school, to pepper him with homework questions that had stumped them the night before. Joey, at 16, was not fully-grown, so the bunch that walked him to school hid him. It's fun to have a brother who's a genius, which is what people were always saying. Max used to brag that they bought Joey a chemistry set when he was 11 and he burned a hole in the floor, making an acid out of sugar or something. You would have thought he had discovered aluminum. But he had been a special favorite of Mrs. Holt, the high school chemistry teacher.

In his high School yearbook, Joey was called "a mathematical wizard." And he worked in the store alongside all those other heroes of mine, the guys in their white coats and white aprons.

Joey was a hero, but Sylvia, the only daughter, 13, flamboyant and defiant, was much more of an influence on me than Joey. She was referred to as "stocky," meaning overweight. She was also beautiful, and ran with an entertaining gang of teen-age Jewish girls from central casting. There was every type, including the actress, the comic, and even twins. They had a club and had blue-and-white plaid jackets with "Entre Nous" in big script on the back.

Sid was fun to have around, the "baby" with the attention that went with that. But he was also always trotting to keep up, and sometimes felt left out. At a very young age, he said, "No one tells me anything."

Downstairs were the landlords, Mr. and Mrs. Meltz. I witnessed what I believe was the only do-it-yourself project of Max's life. He was nailing down a brass strip joining two pieces of linoleum in the kitchen. Someone knocked on the kitchen door and I opened it.

Standing there was Mrs. Meltz's black maid, a quiet, gentle lady. "Mr. Bennett, Mrs. Meltz says could you bang a little softer." Max, on his knees, takes a beat, then he says, "Yeah, tell her I'm gonna buy a rubber hammer."

For me, early Sundays were the best, with boys in boxer shorts wandering around wading through all the Sunday papers, especially the comic strip sections. And the food: Max would suddenly appear after some Sunday religious service carrying big Kraft paper bags full of all kinds of goodies.

In the store, especially, Max moved with a great easy confidence, busy with his own thoughts, and you would catch him humming. You would swear that he didn't even see you as he came out of the walk-in cooler and passed you, carrying one of his beautifully arranged white porcelain trays of pork chops and slipping it into the glass case out front. This sort of concentration was a family trait. I was often sent to get Joey for supper, and would find him on the living room carpet, reading. I would have to bend over and yell in his ear to get his attention.

Max looked like the happiest man in Everett, maybe in Massachusetts, maybe in the whole United States. He was always buoyant, not morose like many of the other immigrant families, even though they had every reason to be the way they were.

Why not? He had arrived in Boston from Lithuania in 1906, an immigrant Jewish boy of 14 with ten dollars in his pockets. He had stayed with relatives named Fishtine in the West End of Boston for two weeks, knowing every minute he had to get out and get a job.

His first job was for $2.50 a week, including room and board. His first dozen or so jobs were in Jewish grocery stores, but he was determined to get into "American" stores, meaning English-speaking, and gradually rose in salary, and acquired various skills, including meat cutting. He was raised from fifteen dollars a week to sixteen when he got married, but he was burning to own his first store, and it happened right after he married Lillian.

He had taught himself to read and write English, and now, 28 years after arriving in Boston, he owned a successful store in hustling, bustling Everett Square, and had a son in Harvard. No one had gotten into Harvard from Everett in 10 years, let alone someone Jewish, and here Joey and George Oshry, son of a friend of Max's, and also Jewish, had made it. The high school hierarchy had told them don't even try. Max said, "Anything is possible in America." He meant positive things, but he also said it derisively about things like the Ponzi scheme. "How can people be so foolish?"

Max had a slight accent. He had married quite a catch in 1917, an "American" girl who was a talented bookkeeper at 18, a Chelsea High School graduate who had arrived in America from Russia at age four and so had no accent.

Sidney, at four, was a charming, square-built little guy, eager to please people, and famous in the family for his bravery when he had about a quarter-inch of the ring finger on his right hand chopped off by the sharp-edged handle of a toy wagon. He was taken up the hill to the Whidden Hospital, and didn't cry or complain when they stitched him up. With the big gap in ages, Sid and I were sort of a second family, well taken care of, but benefitting from almost total freedom to do what we wanted. I think Max and Lil, like parents traditionally, had used up a lot of nervous energy on Joe and Syl, so they were more relaxed with Sid and me.

Sid, already the budding family comic at age four, was exasperatingly telling knock-knock jokes. Worse, he made up some of them. In the summer of 1934, on the ferry from Boston to Nantasket Beach, the crew had arranged chairs on the aft deck, and asked for volunteer entertainers.

Sid got up and said, "Knock-knock."

The delighted crowd yelled, "Who's there?"

"Light-man."

"Light man who?"

"Light-man, put out the light."

Everybody laughed and cheered. What do you suppose that does to the mind of a four-year-old? To be fair, he got much funnier later.

Now, in 1934, Max was in the store for four years that would stretch to two decades. He owned his own store, was making a living and making him more of an American. Not bad. To me, he was the most exuberant immigrant; aware every day of what he had here, coupled with an awareness of the terrible life he had escaped.

He had been through the crash, when he had a store on Main Street in Everett, and there were vague stories about him making a lot of money in the 1920's, and owning several triple-deckers, the All-American wooden three-story dwellings, which were intertwined with our lives forever.

The crash was marked photographically in our family. There were family pictures taken in downtown Boston photo studios, with Joey, Sylvia, Max, and Lillian grouped in formal, old-fashioned poses. There is one of me alone, taken in 1927 when I was one year old. But Sidney was born in 1930 and I guess the money was getting tight, because there is no studio photo of him.

I was brought home to a triple-decker on Main Street when I was born, and Sidney was brought home to the same place four years later. Triple-deckers were the plain, unaffected workingmen's dwellings, maybe more precisely the immigrant's dwelling. Many of them were built by groups of immigrants working cooperatively, from about 1880 to 1930. About 30,000 of them were built, in Maine, Rhode Island, and Massachusetts, in Worcester, Brockton, and mainly, Boston and suburbs, where they evolved from blue-collar housing to ultimately attract yuppies, baby boomers, and professionals.

Triple-deckers evolved in appreciation, too, at least at the rate of the economy. A triple-decker built for a thousand dollars in 1900, condominiumized late in the same century, might fetch $250,000 for each floor.

Triple-deckers have always fascinated me because I believe, unlike any other type of mass construction, they are 100% American. Surprisingly, they are mostly ignored by the groves of academe. The major exceptions are the studies, essentially sociological, done by Arthur J. Krim of the Boston Redevelopment Authority, in which the author's affection for triple-deckers is tangible.

Boston architects, I believe, are snobbish about triple-deckers. Probably because they were just built by workingmen, and not really designed by anyone. Later, architects got in on the act and added attractive and also unattractive details. Their indifference seems odd because a triple-decker might be ideal housing to fit in a small space where communities don't want large-scale apartment buildings. Boston and all its suburbs have spaces where a triple-decker would fit right in, and on the footprint of a single-family house, create three homes.

The triple-decker could not be simpler. A three-story wooden structure with one "flat" or apartment on each floor, it could hold several big immigrant families, or later, single people, couples, or small families. All three floors have front and back porches, but the family on the first floor might be cheated a little on the front porch, because it is the entrance for all three floors. It's an efficient sort of building, especially for the northeast, because the three flats warm each other. The layouts vary from modest to generous, and the porches add storage space, sitting space, and a place to sleep on hot summer nights. Over the years, many porches were closed in to add rooms. On all four sides, there are windows for lots of air and lots of light, much more than an apartment house dwelling of the same size. And the most anyone has to climb is two flights plus the stairs up to the front porch entrance.

On Vine Street in Everett, in the middle floor of a triple-decker, our flat was big enough to have a corridor with rooms on both sides and when you got to the kitchen you could come back through the dining room and living room. Perfect for running like a maniac through the house, or for chasing your brother.

I was listening to the radio and ducking bedtime. Max was still up. Sid was asleep. Syl had left the house with some girlfriends.

This was the setting for the wildest scene starring Max that I ever witnessed. Max was never violent, but he looked like he might get there that night.

What I saw, suddenly, through my eight-year-old eyes, was Max, holding a wooden kitchen chair high over his head, with the legs sticking up. He was chasing his oldest son through the flat, and angry, as if he were going to kill Joey.

And yet, even at eight, I was calm with the instinct that everything was going to be all right.

My mother, sitting, kept saying, not loudly, "Max. Max. Max. Max."

It took about one loop of the flat for him to stop and sit down, breathing hard, and for garbled agitated talk between him and Lillian in Yiddish.

Later I found out that Joey was not only enrolled at Harvard, but also at Yeshiva (Hebrew College) and was saying he wanted to drop Yeshiva.

Yeshiva was the older idea, long taken for granted by Max. Harvard had become a reality during Joey's senior year in high school.

When I was told about it later and understood it, I thought it was nuts. It was like asking someone to go to Harvard and Yale at the same time. Joey had started both and discovered it was too much.

Sounds reasonable to me.

In fact, you can't help wondering why anyone thought it would work. Probably because Joey was unbelievably smart. And probably because anything is possible in America. Joey must have had an inkling it was wrong, but he started the two colleges anyway and then saw it was impossible.

I always loved that he had the stuff to assert himself at 16.

As for Max, at 42, it unraveled him and he had to make a big adjustment. Who knows what he was thinking as he sat there staring across the room and recovering his breathing? He must have faced up to the fact that Joey would never become a rabbi. And probably neither of the other two sons would either. Well, that was part of the price of assimilation into America, no? But hadn't he done the same thing to his own father?

When he was eleven in the old country, hadn't he used up the local Hebrew School teaching talent of his hometown of Aran?

And hadn't he been sent 40 miles away to a Yeshiva in Vilna, which was called the Jerusalem of Lithuania, because it had a dozen Yeshivas and two dozen synagogues?

And hadn't he come home one day to Aran when he was 14 and told his father that he did not want to continue on the road to become a rabbi?

Was he being punished for quitting Yeshiva?

Was he being punished for working in his store on Saturday? No, he didn't believe in the harsh and vengeful God of the Old Testament.

He had startled everybody one day by announcing that he thought God was Nature.

He had loved Yeshiva. He left Lithuania because he'd been disgusted by the ugly things he saw, like Cossacks carelessly trampling people to death under their horses, with no repercussions. He wasn't afraid of the Cossacks. I think he was fearless, but the second-class status of the Jews, the conditions in Lithuania, basically insulted his intelligence.

So that, with the limited choices of occupations for Jews, and endless discussions of what to do with him, finally the only decision he would go along with was that he would try to find a new life in America.

And hadn't America been worth it all?

1892 David

On January 15, 1892, my father is born in the small town of Aran (renamed Varena), Lithuania, while under the flag of the Russian Tzar.

His father Avram runs to get Rebecca the midwife, but the baby is already born when they get back, Rebecca cuts the umbilical cord and is a big help to Shaina the mother.

The baby is their seventh child and first boy. The first four babies died; one is a miscarriage, one at birth, and two as infants.

After the death of the fourth child, Avram and Shaina traveled on a horse and wagon to the city of Oshmene, where there was a well-known "Good Jew." They believed in the blessings of a good, just and pious Jew. Shaina received the blessing, returned to Aran, and never lost another baby.

Two sisters were born before my father, Michle and Chaya. The two older sisters are eager to make a fuss over him.

Now there is a son, a strapping baby with a big chest and a noisy, lusty cry, which is easily muffled at his mother's breast. From sturdy dark Shaina he inherits a white porcelain complexion and from his father, tall and rugged Avram, he inherits his curly black hair.

They are struggling the same as everyone else, but they're not poor. Avram has a good job at one of the local lumberyards; in fact, he is second man to Schaeffer, the owner, and his pay is twenty rubles a month. In addition, he brings home all the logs needed for winter heating and cooking year-round, plus finished lumber for repairs and additions on the house.

Avram is also something of a linguist in a time when there are at least eight languages spoken in the area: Russian, Lithuanian, Polish, German, Yiddish, Latvian, Estonian, and Finnish. Avram can get along in all of them.

The Tzar is in the business of selling forests at government auctions and Avram earns money on the side bidding for the trees for his boss and for others, and also at auctions of horses and cows and goats.

Last names, surnames, have only recently come into use. Jews especially didn't need them. You were so-and-so, son of so-and-so, from such-and-such a place. But Avram has a last name… Beniatovich. An odd name, because it seems to mean son of son of.

So at the little boy's briss (circumcision), eight days after his birth, he is named Mordecai ben Avram Aran Beniatovich. Avram and his friend Schechter, holding the baby for the ritual razor cuts of the circumcision by the moyel (the Rabbi who performs the ceremony), are amazed at the strength of the protesting boy, and each is terrified for a moment that he might lose his hold. The moyel coolly detaches his little silver vise-like instrument from the baby's bloody penis and swaddles him with some white cotton handed to him by Shaina.

"Mottke" is the diminutive of Mordecai, and it's a nickname that will last for a long time.

<u>1893</u>

A third daughter is born to Avram and Shaina, and her name is Rachel, but there are no inroads on Mottke's psyche. He is still picked up and kissed on both cheeks daily, morning and night, by Avram, and hugged and kissed by his mother and by his sisters. And there is plenty of the same kind of attention from Avram's parents, Zaydie (grandfather) Yosel and Buhbbie (grandmother) Hinde who come mornings two or three times a week for services at the shul (synagogue). They prize all the children, but there is something about lively, darting, smart little Mottke that attracts most of their attention. He is swept up by them and smothered with kisses that he remembers the rest of his life.

In Eisiskes, a nearby town, Zaydie had been a brick maker, but in Aran all he does is go to shul three times a day.

These are Mottke's only grandparents. Shaina's parents died when she was young and she doesn't remember them.

Life is good, Mottke is allowed to run free, and he runs everywhere. He can't get into much trouble on these dirt roads in this small town, with one exception, which he learns quickly. One does not go out on certain roads on each side of town because of the Cossacks, the Tzar's horse soldiers. They race at reckless speed whenever they feel like it, and slash with their sabers, too, and just trample someone to injury or to death every so often. There is never any follow-up to these deaths.

<u>1895</u>

Buhbbie dies. But Zaydie Yosel still comes to visit regularly and is a fixture on Passover, when Mottke recites the Four Questions at the Seder dinners. It falls to Mottke because, in the custom, of the time, as the youngest male who can, to ask the questions about the celebrations of the Exodus of the Jews from Egypt.

<u>1897</u>

A second son is born, named Nathan. Everyone says he is a twin of Mottke, who is too busy at five to pay much attention to the new baby. Mottke is running with a gang of five and six year olds, up and down the streets of Aran, which are endlessly entertaining. It's tea with milk in it for breakfast, along with a roll or bagel with some butter on it, and the explorers are off on their daily adventure.

Writing notes about his childhood 75 years later, Mottke has an extraordinary memory of his hometown.

There are three synagogues, and Mottke's crowd is in and out of all of them. There was one old shul and one new shul and a shul for the young folks, a shvitzbud (sweat bath house) where adults go for a weekly steam bath, the men usually on Shabbos (Sabbath) night, when they might occasionally take a son along. There are separate days for women and girls, when no men are allowed. There is a sort of bed and breakfast for wayfarers. They do a lot of business, and there are a lot of characters at the inn for the boys to watch arriving and parting. There is a Rabbi, two shamuses or sextons, one Cantor and one understudy Cantor (!). There are five private Hebrew schools in the teacher's homes, and a school for poor children.

There are: one constable, one town watchman, a liquor store, a post office, a Roman Catholic church, two wells, two ponds, two rivers, a bridge over the larger river and a railroad station on the other side, three bakeries: one Jewish, one non-Jewish, and one pastry (once in a while they get a roll each or a cookie), four woolen goods and fabric stores, a men's ready-made-suit store, a women's ready-made-dress store, two pharmacies, three meat markets, a beer-only saloon, an attorney, a painter/whitewasher, a tinsmith/coppersmith, a flour store, a cap store and a hat store, a bookbinder, four lumberyards, a paper mill, a starch factory, a blacksmith, four shoemakers, one custom cap maker, three men's tailors, two women's dressmakers, one pottery maker, a cemetery, a tea room, and a dairyman who brings milk, cheese and butter three times a week.

There is a weekly public market the day after Shabbos, when peasants bring poultry, eggs, potatoes, carrots, cabbages, turnips, all kinds of vegetables, fruit, and even calves and cows and horses and goats.

Aran is not a typical Lithuanian town. The farmers' markets all over the country are scanty in goods and sell out quickly.

Aran's weekly market is heavily stocked and lasts all day. The bustling town is filled with people who can buy.

Army and cavalry officers and enlisted men and some of their wives attend, too.

There is something different about Aran, something that makes it uniquely secure economically. That something is the huge army post right outside of town. Noisy maneuvers are held every summer, and the town is filled with uniforms every day.

The Tzar's officers buy lumber from all four lumberyards for the constant building of barracks and fences, and also refined wooden items such as rails and rail holders for training the Cossacks' horses to jump.

All of these people and buildings fascinate Mottke and his crowd and they explore constantly. They seem to know they only have a year or two left before they have to start Chayder, the Hebrew language elementary school, a couple hours a day, four days a week. So they are busy all the time cataloging the town. In the winter there is ice and snow on the frozen ground, and in the spring - mud. There is only one main street, with 12 cross streets with no names.

One day, Mottke and his friends are hanging around outside on the porch of the tearoom and five Cossacks ride up and tie their horses to the hitching rail. They are all blue and brown wool and big lapels and gold epaulets and brass buttons and boots that come up high over their knees and lower in back. Their sabers clang and clunk hitting the floor as they sprawl in their seats in the tearoom chairs. They order tea and Yosel the Tea Man brings five steaming glasses on a tray, each glass in a saucer. Also in each saucer is a cube of sugar and a long spoon. Yosel's wife brings a tray with five pieces of yellow cake. The Cossacks drop their cubes into the tea and stir.

The boys are silent watching every detail through the open doors.

One of the Cossacks calls over Yosel, "Hey, what about more sugar, my tea's not sweet enough."

Yosel says, "No, you only get one cube. I saw you, you stirred too hard."

The Cossack accepts what Yosel says.

The boys are punching each other and grabbing at each other and rolling off the porch, stifling giggles and laughter. The Cossacks are stupid! You stirred it too hard!

When Mottke tells Avram and Shaina about it later, Avram says, "What did you think, they were trained at the military academy in Moscow? They're mostly farm boys, taken off the farm, drafted, because someone thought they might look good on a horse."

About Aran, Mottke comments, "You could call it on the literary side." Not surprising, considering that Aran is only 40 miles from Vilna the city that is called "the Jerusalem of Lithuania" because of the passion for learning, learning, learning, the language, the Bible, the Talmud. In Vilna, there are a dozen synagogues and five Yeshivas, or Hebrew Colleges.

Zaydie dies. Mottke misses him intensely for a while, and then less intensely, but still, for the rest of his life.

*****

Mordecai is nine years old and starts Chayder. His teacher and the family all know right away that he is very bright. He is also respectful and dutiful.

Friday afternoons before Shabbos, he is busy going from house to house with a blue-and-white cardboard can with a slit on top, to collect money for different charities and for Palestine. He keeps an accounting in a notebook and Avram helps him at the end of the day as they turn the money over to the people who are in charge of it.

After that is the Shabbos eve ritual of benching licht, or lighting the candles, by Shaina, with a shawl or a kerchief over her head. Shaina has a prized silver candelabra from her side of the family that holds five candles. This is the style of the Litvaks, or Lithuanians. There are many other sects of Jews, with other customs. The Rushashuh, or Russians, tend to have three separate candles, and the Galitzyanah from Poland light on one candle. These styles and others are represented in Aran.

As Shaina waves her hands over the candles and brings her hands together while she recites the blessing, Mottke is enthralled by the mystic ceremony, just as his mother enthralls him. Not only does he love her and respect her for all the cooking and cleaning and sewing, he knows she is the only mother in Aran who works as hard as she does.

She buys limestone from whoever brings it to her, and bakes it into powder in her extra stoves. She is the only one in Aran with three stoves in the kitchen. She and Avram bag the limestone in flour sacks they buy from the general store, and when they have a wagonload, take it to the army camp, where they buy all she can bring for cement, for plating, and for whitewash.

After the candles is the best meal of the week. Often it is a pot roast that has been cooking most of the day in Shaina's biggest pot. There is an abundance of potatoes, carrots and turnip, and a soupy liquid that is paradise to Mottke. It's salty and peppery, a thick rich brown sauce, and the store-brought braided challah dipped into it is indescribable.

The fabulous meat has cooked for so long that it shreds as it is served. Then there is a thick green pea soup. Every meal ends with soup, even when the main part of the meal is soupy.

*****

Mordecai is eleven and has exhausted what the elementary school can provide, so Avram finds "a learned man," a teacher with no children in Olenek, a neighboring town, for teaching Mottke, with room included, but not board. For food, it's arranged that he eat every day with a different friend of Avram's. He lives this way for a whole year. He comes home for Yom Kippur and Rosh Hashonah, and for Passover.

*****

Mottke tells Avram he wants to go to the big city, Vilna, to one of the Yeshivas. Avram is delighted; nothing would make him happier than to have a Rabbi in the family. The language, the words, the Bible, constantly energizes Mottke; the Talmud once in a while. He has always been enthusiastic about everything that crosses his path.

Once he gets to Vilna, he is not a bit homesick. Mottke is the youngest of the Yeshiva bochers (college boys), who uncomplainingly sleep in their overcoats in the pews of the Yeshiva shul, using their soft travel bags for pillows. The shamus finds the boys places to eat at a different Vilna home almost every night. Sometimes a housewife, wanting to skip a night of serving the boys, gives them each five or ten kopecks. The boys like this; it's plenty for a meal and gives them pocket money besides.

A government order comes down; the Tzar has decided everyone will learn the Russian language, even the second-class Jews. So the Yeshiva boys find themselves going to Government-run schools two hours a day, three times week. Mottke dives into this new language just the way he did Hebrew. There is nothing negative about it to him.

*****

One Shabbos morning in January, Mottke tells the Sexton at the Yeshiva shul that he is thirteen years old, and needs to be called up for an Aliyah, or blessing, in front of the congregation, so he can consider himself bar mitzvahed. The Sexton tells Mottke he can't work him in, there are too many congregants scheduled to receive the honors, but he will take care of Mottke at Mincha, the pre-sundown service.

In the late afternoon, the Sexton calls Mottke up to the bima (altar) for an Aliyah, and "I became a full-fledged Jew."

One Shabbos morning in June, Mottke goes with three fellow students to the big synagogue in Vilna because a famous Cantor named Sirotin is performing the service. The shul is overflowing, including the balcony, which is filled with women and their daughters.

Everything seems as usual. In the serene atmosphere of the shul, the two Torahs are taken from the ark at the back of the bima. A small procession carries the Torahs; in their elaborately embroidered red velvet covers, down the aisle of the shul and back to the altar, and congregants who can reach them, touch the Torahs with their shawls and then kiss the shawl where it touched the Torah. One of the Torahs is uncovered and spread on the huge table on the bima, and the two spools spread so that the day's reading can be found.

Sirotin's big baritone fills every corner of the big shul as he sings the words of the Torah. Mottke is dazzled and everyone is thrilled. They've never heard anyone like him.

All Cantors are different. There is a guide for singing in the symbols under the calligraphy of the Torah, but there are many sects of Jews with variations on interpretation, not to mention the personal style of the sometimes-gigantic ego of the individual cantor.

The cantor is finished and the Torah is returned to the ark. The service continues, and then the Sexton is reading the blessings of the Shabbos. Men are being called up individually to receive an Aliyah.

Now the Sexton is starting the customary blessing for the Tzar, and Mottke sees a dozen young men jump up and run up the steps of the bima, shouting in protest to stop the Sexton.

Mottke is momentarily puzzled by some peculiar moving spots of light on the east wall of the shul, and all in the same instant, sees Cossack sabers reflecting the sun, and dozens of Cossacks pouring into the jammed synagogue, slashing. Spattering's of blood are everywhere; they hit the front of the ark and the men on the bima, and some of the congregants. Young men are being slashed and maimed, and beat up and arrested. The women and girls in the balcony are screaming.

Mottke, writing about it 75 years later: "We jumped out of the windows and are still running. That will be in my mind as long as I will live, when the Cossacks were slashing from left to right and maiming almost everybody."

Mottke feels he has been innocent, foolish, simple, even though he saw people killed by careless Cossacks when he was a little boy in Aran. He had thought of these events as accidents that you just had to accept and go on. Now for the first time he is interested in the political realities. He begins to read some of the socialist pamphlets and literature that are in plentiful supply. Poets write longingly about owning their own land and farming it, denied to them in Lithuania and Russia. He remembers a friend of his father who fled the country - he just left his wife and a house full of children one night and disappeared.

Last summer the Yeshiva boys were given the use of a house and he remembers one night being woken up by the other boys, who sensed they were going to be raided by Cossacks.

"We have to move out right now." And the house was raided.

When Mottke goes home for the holidays in the fall, he doesn't tell his parents about the riot in the shul, but he tells them how he became bar mitzvahed. He tells Avram truthfully that he doesn't like Vilna and asks can he go to Yeshiva somewhere else. Avram and Mottke agree he will go to a Yeshiva in Lido. Shaina packs up a soft bag for him and he takes the train to Lido.

He is supposed to change in Vilna to a train for Lido, but the trains have stopped running and people are darting about and shouting. It turns out there is a general railroad strike through Lithuania.

Mottke walks down to Zavalno Street to a small restaurant near the station and finds a wagon-driver from Warenova who has picked up merchandise in Vilna and is returning. Mottke knows Warenova is on the way to Lido and asks for a ride.

They start in the late afternoon and it soon gets chilly. But the wagon man has quilts and blankets to keep them warm and they arrive in Warenova early in the morning. The man has learned Mottke's story during the night and says Mottke can stay with him until the trains start up or he finds a ride to Lido.

Mottke is relieved to not be stranded in Vilna. It turns out the wagon driver has a big house and he tells Mottke there is a Chayder operating in part of it. Everyone is asleep in the house when they arrive. Mottke is given a room and gratefully falls asleep.

Mottke wakes up midday and a nice woman in the kitchen gives him some tea with milk and a piece of dark break with butter. Nosing around, he looks in on the Chayder, and gets "the biggest surprise in my young life." It's his old teacher from Aran, Rachavke.

Rachavke also advises him to stay until the trains are running again, and meanwhile go to shul and study by himself. Rachavke says there are "high learned men" at the shul and they will help Mottke. Mottke starts on this plan, but for the first time, he is not industrious. "But I will admit it did not work out very good and I got mixed up with the young socialists."

Some of these are the communists who will take over Russia in 1917.

One night Mottke is with a small group who walk to a linen factory in Warenova where the workers are being kept late night after night, without being paid for the extra hours to finish a job of table covers and napkins for the palace of the Tzar.

Three of them throw rocks and break windows and run. Mottke is one of the rock-throwers. "That was the time I began to think, what it is all about? I started to think, what is this rabbinical stuff that my father wants me to study for? But, now I have seen that I won't go through with it and this is the best time to stop studying and go home and be honest and tell my father."

Mottke arrives home for Chanukah for the first time in four years. Winter has settled on Aran and the ground is frozen with snow covering the streets and the roofs.

"This was the turning point in my life. No more school."

The town constable visits Avram at work one day. He tells Avram that there is a question about whether Mottke was one of the boys in an incident in Warenova, but he trusts that Avram can take care of it. Avram tells Mottke what the constable said, but with no comment and no punishment.

Avram begins to think about a good trade for Mottke to follow. Mottke is in agreement with his father, but the question is, what is a good trade? There are very few jobs open to Jews. Mottke can be sent away to apprentice to a jeweler or a clockmaker. He doesn't want to do that. He can become a tailor, he doesn't want that, either. He can come a furniture maker, a wood carver. Avram knows men who have become furniture maker to the Tzar. Avram travels to Vilna and finds out there is a chance to apprentice to a photographer, and a trade Mottke can enter, painting huge curtains used in the theatres.

Nothing appeals to Mottke, and he knows he is causing pain, but he is trying to be honest. Is he just afraid of sabers? No, he thinks, there is something illogical about this life in Lithuania, something that insults his intelligence.

Avram confers with the Rabbi and some of the village elders, and the answer Avram comes back with is that Mottke should go to America. Mottke is surprised, but something about it sounds right.

Avram is on the edge of crying, but he holds it back. Mottke writes that his father said, "That will be the best thing for you."

Avram finds out how to go about it. The man for the job is an agent named Chazanovich, who knows how to get people over the border from Russia into Germany, and how to buy train tickets there for Rotterdam and a ship to America.

It's decided he will go right after Passover.

Mottke and a few others walk across Lithuania to the German border.

To steal across the border, Mottke and a group of 20, including a few women, are awakened at three o'clock in the morning. Chazanovich's man gets everyone together and leads them on a march. "Not a sound from nobody."

They only walk about a half-mile and Chazanovich's man shouts, "We are over the border!"

"And the next thing we knew we were in a German inn and there was plenty to eat and drink." They take a rest and then board a train for Yatkun where everyone gets a steam bath, and their clothes are sent through steam ovens. Then they board a train for Holland.

Riding through Germany and Holland at some of the stations in the bigger towns, Jewish women come up to the train and give food to the emigrants. There are rolls and bagels with butter on them and hard-boiled eggs. And square pieces of lokshen kugel, a noodle pudding with raisins in it. For small children, the women have cookies and five-pfennig coins.

The reason for the baths is revealed in Rotterdam when they are inspected for cleanliness at the ticket office for the boat. Now they find out there is a two-week wait for a boat.

The 14-year-old has a good time getting to know Rotterdam while waiting for the departure.

Chazanovich has arranged everything for the boat trip. The whole group is booked Third Class, which turns out to be fine with Mottke. There are eight people in a room that holds only two in First and Second Class, but after all, you only sleep in the room, so it's not a hardship. The German and Dutch food is very good and plentiful. Mottke adjusts to food he has never seen before, although whether by concession or accident, some of it is familiar, such as chicken soup with dumplings, and lots of boiled potatoes. The Germans are good at bread, too. There are pumpernickels and ryes, while Sauerbraten and meat pies are new, and enjoyable. He's pretty sure he is eating pork and ham, and figures he has to eat them to survive. The apple strudel is like his mother's, and so is the stuffed cabbage.

The first few days there is too much to eat because so many people are getting seasick that they aren't touching their food. But in a few days everyone feels better.

"Well time flies and in 14 days we were in New York." They see the New York skyline, like nothing in their experience. Mottke is thrilled by the Statue of Liberty but takes it calmly. Some of the Third Class passengers are almost overcome by the sight of the powerful symbol.

But they are landed on Ellis Island, where Mottke finds out Chazanovich is not perfect. When his paper share is looked over by the Immigration officers, they find that Mottke came on a half ticket that says he is 12 years old, and not only that, but the papers are written for two brothers.

The chief translator, Joseph Gyory is summoned to deal with the boy because he can speak Yiddish (in addition to French, Spanish, Italian, English, Slovak, German and from his own heritage, Hungarian). He befriends the boy and helps as much as he can. Mottke manages to get in touch with a cousin named Benny Benetovich in New York, but Benny can't help except to get in touch with Mottke's sponsor, an uncle named Kalman Fishtine, husband of first cousin Rose Beniatovich, from Boston. He comes to Ellis Island, but he can't overcome the bureaucracy either.

Mottke spends six weeks on Ellis Island.

The time is boring but not wasted. Gyory starts him on his first attack on the English language, and brings him a newspaper every day.

He actually has his own room, and the food is generous, even though there is a lot of white bread and thin soup he has never seen before. He becomes friends with some of the Immigration officers, who are predominantly Irish-Americans.

"I got sick of the Statue of Liberty."

Mottke is sent back to Lithuania.

Gyory says goodbye to the boy and says he will look forward to his return.

Mottke travels all the way home to Aran, with a couple of Gyory's newspapers stuffed in his bag, and starts all over.

In Aran, there is consternation when he shows up with his tale. Chazanovich is sent for. He proclaims his innocence and will look into the problem.

Mottke informs his parents that he has not given up the idea of going to America and he wants to go right back.

After a few days of family discussion and advice, they form a plan. This time, instead of using Chazanovich and his methods, they will try a more legal approach. It will cost more, but it will be worth it. The news that Uncle Zalman's daughter Chaike wants to go to America helps firm their decision. Also, Chazanovich returns their money.

Mottke and Chaike are brought to Eisiskes, the nearby town that is the repository for records for Aran. There they will get Russian passports to America. The family tells the officials that they are brother and sister. They say he is sixteen and she is fifteen (he is fourteen and she is thirteen).

They have their papers in a couple of weeks. This time, the farewells are at the train station. They are on their way to Liverpool. Mottke does not want to see the Statue of Liberty again, so they will enter America through Boston, where their American sponsor, Kalman Fishtine, lives.

They leave Liverpool on the S.S. Ivernia on the twenty-first of August and disembark on September 6, 1906.

In Boston, he finds 30 Parmenter Street in the North End and relatives named Fishtine and stays with them for two weeks, traveling into Boston almost every day on the horse-drawn/electric trolley cars.

To the 14-year-Old, not yet fully grown, Boston looks like the little bit of New York that he saw, with horse-drawn carriages and horseless carriages that make his heart skip a beat.

The names of the automobiles are mostly hard to read: Reliance, Studebaker, Aero, Rainier, and Moline. Ford is easy.

And there are thousands of people. It's a wonder they don't get killed crossing the streets. The men are mostly in suits and ties and fedoras and bowlers and there are women rushing to work and rushing home just like the men.

It is pure enjoyment. He can't believe his luck, and the relief after Lithuania, and the three Atlantic crossings, and the six weeks on Ellis Island is palpable. After two weeks of the West End, Max responds eagerly to the automatic pressure that floats in his mind, unarticulated but as sharp as a shard of glass...you have to go to work.

He walks into a grocery Store on Chambers Street and asks for a job. He is hired for $1.75 a week including room and board, and after four weeks asks for a raise and gets it, $2.50 a week.

This is the first of a series of jobs in Jewish grocery Stores. He is a good boy: "I wrote home just what I am doing. I wasn't homesick at any time. I was satisfied it was really a New World."

His letters home are in Yiddish, but he is rapidly learning to read and write in English. All his experiences before are diminished by America.

For a 14-year-old he has seen a lot, but everything in America is different, bigger, more intense. The variety of people is endless and enjoyable and he interacts easily. Everyone likes the stocky, red-cheeked handsome, smiling, exuberant boy. There are dozens of places where he feels he could walk in and get a job. He figures he is probably not equipped to go into those jobs in the big buildings, but it doesn't matter. There are plenty here for him. He likes moving stock in the stores, waiting on people, and best of all, getting outdoors to make a delivery.

There seem to be all kinds of possibilities. In fact, anything seems possible in America. His relatives acquaint him with the Forward, the English-language newspaper for the Jewish community, concerned especially with helping immigrants get along in their new country. Some fellow workers are excited by the October 6th Forward, in which there is a story and an editorial about a 17-year-old Jewish boy who is the first winner of the Newsboys Union Scholarship to Harvard College.

By now, Max knows what Harvard College is. Almost 300 years old, and just one of several colleges in the area. Boston is a Vilna, passionately, busily committed to learning, learning, learning. And 17-year-Old Meyer Heller is going to Harvard.

In the Same October 6th paper is a story about anti-Semitism in Malden. Well, so there is anti-Semitism in America, but no Cossacks. At least, no Tzar's Cossacks.

He leaves his first job on Chambers Street and gets a new job on Parkman Street for $3.00 a week and a more comfortable homey place to live. Now he can buy some shirts and shoes and warmer clothes as winter closes in. He stays on this job a whole year.

*****

Next he gets a job for six dollars a week in a bigger store on Laurel Street and stays for about a year and a half.

The next job he gets is in a bakery plant, delivering bread and rolls to stores in Roxbury and Blue Hill Avenue in Mattapan.

This time he doesn't like the cold and rain and snow of the outdoors, and doesn't like meeting only very few people.

So he quits and gets a job in a grocery store on the corner of Cambridge and Grove Streets. This is his first jump into a store where there is a new trend, a Jewish owner who speaks English, and where all the customers speak English, which is very important to Max.

But when school closes in June, the owner brings his son into the store and lets Max go. He lands a bakery job again. This time it's a rough job delivering bread and rolls to stores in the West End, with a wagon and a team of horses.

The catch is there are three deliveries a day, 2AM, 10AM, and 3PM.

"But I worked there until I got something else."

The "something else" is an opportunity Max is eager for. "I happened to know a man who was a partner in The American Grocery Company so I asked him if he could get me in to work there and he did. This was a wholesale place and that was just what I wanted so I could learn real business."

In fact, he wants it badly enough to take a cut to $5 a week, which by now is not enough to live on, because he has to pay his own room and board. But he wants it enough to put up with the problems, because he is learning. After a couple months, he asks one of the bosses, named Mr. Gilkoff, for a raise, and goes to $6 a week.

1910

Max interrupts his narrative to confess, "I will stop now and say I wasn't writing home too often but I wrote sometimes." It's now four years since he left home and he receives letters from his sisters and his father. There is some resentment that Nathan doesn't add anything to the letters.

Nathan, nine years old when Max left, is thirteen now, and has never been away from home as Max was. Doesn't Nathan have plenty of time to add some regards to one of the sister's letters?

What Max has no way of knowing is that Nathan's mind is filled with a passion that Max never experienced. He is reading all the same socialist pamphlets and poetry that Max read, but unlike Max, he knows exactly what he wants to do. He is on fire to be a farmer, and he knows where he wants to be one - in Palestine.

*****

"In 1910 there was a slogan - Go West, young man." By this time, the 18-year old has several non-Jewish friends.

"Now I began to talk to my best pals to go to California and they were thinking the same thing. And one day we packed up and started out to go. We got to Battle Creek, Michigan, May 29th.

"We got to a rooming house. It was a very cold day for May and the landlord had to make the furnace." The next day is Memorial Day so they look around the City, and watch the parade.

There are lots of factories - Maple Flakes, Quaker Oats, Kellogg's and Post Toasties, among others. In fact, Battle Creek is the cereal capital of the world and there are plenty of jobs, so after the holiday, they go to work.

Max and one pal go to Kellogg's, and the other three go to Post Toasties. They are working 10-hour days, and making a lot of money. Max's job is packing individual boxes of cereal into big cardboard cartons and sealing the big box.

The hours are 10 a day and it's a 5 1/2 day week, so it's 55 hours for $10.50 a week. "In comparison to six dollars a week for 11 hour days and a full six days" back in Boston. Then there was a flurry of extra work for a few weeks and Max made as much as 28 dollars a week "but that did not last very long."

Since, in 1910, Americans ate cold cereals only in the summer the Post Toasties friends lose their jobs and take off for Chicago.

Two weeks later Max and his Kellogg's friend follow, but they have lost track of the others. Max can't get work and then one morning "there is an ad for a grocery boy." He runs up to Fullerton Avenue in Chicago and tells the owner of his experience. He is hired for six dollars a week including room and board.

Max's pal also gets work and everything is fine but Max's boss has a daughter who is "nice and good-looking" and she and Max "began to be friendly" but the boss notices and "that was the end of my job."

He has the address of a cousin, son of a brother of his mothers, and writes to him in Racine, Wisconsin, asking, "Does the cousin think Max can find work there?"

The cousin answers, right away, inviting Max to come and live with him and maybe he can find work. This doesn't pan out and after two weeks of trying, Max heads back east to Malden, Massachusetts.

*****

His new job is his first serious encounter with meat cutting. It's a grocery and meat store and the pay is six dollars a week with room and board, and a chance at a meat-cutting lesson every so often. He buys some new clothes, and feels pretty good about getting back into the old groove again.

*****

He stays about a year and it ends when he asks for a raise and is refused. So he quits and finds a job for twelve dollars a week, no room and board, still an advance because room and board is only six dollars a month.

*****

Max becomes ill, is sick, and has his appendix removed. Ten days in the hospital and four days at home and he is back at work.

Romance enters Max's life, and surely there is a part here for Barbara Stanwyck.

He runs into a girl who lives in the North End and whom he knows from Aran, and he remembers that her family was poor. She is dark and pretty and a little wistful-looking, but she really brightens up when Max is around.

Max thinks she is nice, but someone else from Aran, a man named Elke Karpels, tells him, "she is not the girl for me to keep company," even though Max cannot see anything wrong with her.

He's advancing as a meat-cutter at this time, after getting a job at a mainstream meat market in Malden, "a nice place to work".

Max is invited to a birthday party, asks the girl from Aran if she'd like to go with him, and she thanks him, yes, she would.

"But I knew she had no dress to go to a party so I got her a lavender dress and I must say myself she looked beautiful."

They have a good time; he takes her home to the North End, and returns to his room in Malden.

The very next morning a letter arrives from Aran, telling him the family has heard he is dating this girl from Aran, and to stop it "if I want them to live quietly without any heartaches, and do it right away before it is too late."

This is not pleasant news, but Max puts it together with what Elke Karpels had said to him and decides she is not the girl for him.

Max sees her a few more times, but finally he stops. "In time I stopped meeting her and seeing her. It wasn't as easy as writing about it, but I did it and it was over."

*****

"This is now 1914 and I am 22 years old and so I stopped to think about girls and I was happy."

What he thinks about most is having his own store. What preoccupies him is his brother's silence. Still irritated by the lack of correspondence, he is surprised to find out from people from Aran that Nathan, now 17, has emigrated to Palestine. A couple weeks later he gets letters from his sisters with the news, and that his mother "is sick over it."

But why wasn't she "sick over it" when Max traveled to America?

Now 24, Max is still working in the same Malden store, for 15 dollars a week. He is "fixed up" with a girl from Chelsea, and they are dazzled by each other.

She is Lillian Ruth Kaplan, short and dramatic, with unbelievably black hair, which is unbelievably silky, and the smartest girl he has met in America, bar none. He is the smartest man she has met, too, even though she has dated a lot, including owners of sizeable businesses. And the best looking, bar none. Smart as she is, she is incredibly innocent, even for the times. She wears gloves on dates, because she believes you can get pregnant from touching bare hands. She makes money, too, which is very unusual in the immigrant community, Jewish or otherwise, since not many of her generation are able to get an education. Lillian is a high school graduate with a job as a bookkeeper in Boston. She was only four when her family arrived in America, and she has no foreign accent. Max has a slight accent that he will have all his life.

According to some speech specialists, arrive in a new country before puberty, no accent. Arrive after puberty, accent.

*****

Now he's 25 and he and Lillian are married on January 30, 1917. Max gets a one-dollar raise upon getting married. "We were happy but living with my in-laws in Chelsea." Lillian's father Paul is a junkie. That's what someone who owns a junkyard was called. The junkyard is in the small factory section of Chelsea, in a row of junkyards.

Max has never stopped thinking about going into business for himself and "so as it happened after we were married I bought a store in Everett that was a beautiful store with a full line of groceries and meats. I used to say that my wife was my luck."

Traditionally, a young man buying a business might get some help from a father-in-law, but Paul won't, or most likely, can't help. So Max starts by using the other tradition, getting a partner who can put some or all of the cash, and buying him out as soon as possible. This is a high-wire act without a net, the first in a series of store acquisitions with partners who were apparently not too greedy, because several times Max was able to buy them out in a year. Of course, it could easily have gone the other way. And of course, he must be given credit for an ability to size up a store before buying in.

He opens on April 10, 1917. A few months later, the United States enters the war against Germany, and conscription begins. On Christmas morning, Lillian gives birth to a son whom they name Joseph.

*****

In January, Max is 26, and has to report to the draft board. Joseph turns out to be his exemption from service.

*****

The Main Street Market does well. Max buys out his partner.

In 1920 Lillian presents him with a daughter, Irene Sylvia. Max goes into real estate. In 1926 they have a boy, David. Max is getting to be known in the business and Jewish community. He and the bank own three three-deckers and the store.

*****

1929 spoils the American Dream.

In 1930 another boy, Sidney is born.

In 1931 Max has to leave the Main Street store and is able to rent a small store on Norwood Street. He is not there very long when he is forced to move to a different store on Norwood Street. Finally, in 1933 he moves to 15 Norwood Street where he stays until 1950.

Is It Fresh?

David

Max had a phenomenal reputation for fresh fish. People came to the Norwood Market in Everett from towns on the other side of Boston, from Newton, Cambridge, and Waltham. Why? Surely they could buy good fish nearer to where they lived, but maybe it would have been more work to shop for it, maybe they would have had to be better shoppers, maybe they had the common experience of buying fish that was "off" once in a while. Even nowadays most people can't judge fish. In Everett, as in most of the Boston area, there were a lot of Catholics, who in those pre-WWII days observed meatless Fridays. So there was a whole lot of fish eating going on. But most people - it made them a little nervous - approached fish gingerly. So at the same time that there was a lot of eating fish, there was also a lot of ducking fish. Macaroni and cheese was popular.

In fact, macaroni and cheese was the first packaged "dinner" anywhere and 800,000,000 packages were sold in 1937, the year it was introduced, surprising the manufacturers. There were concoctions that some of my Catholic friends recall with a shudder, such as a mixture of canned tuna, fish, peas, carrots and Thousand-Island dressing. There were recipes that mixed fish with other things, like mashed potatoes, and disguised the fact that you were eating fish. Fishcakes are made with salt cod, which was reliable, but a little extra work what with all the soaking required.

There were store-bought meals. Eddie Gold's delicatessen, just three doors up Norwood Street from Norwood Market, sold a lot of fish and chips, the batter-coated, deep-fried fish with French fries. We sold a few somewhat exotic items ourselves to people desperate for something they could tolerate. These included shelled oysters and shelled clams, which we got in gallon cans and dispensed in cardboard pint and half-pint containers. They were straight-sided cylinders, not conical like modern coffee containers. In fact, they were also used by us as coffee take-out containers and were stronger, more enjoyable, more secure than the current ones. Another item was smoked finnan haddie, beautiful orange-colored smoked fillets that came in wood boxes from Nova Scotia.

Two revolutions came along in the attitudes towards fish. First was WWII and rationing. Whether you liked fish or not, fish became attractive to everyone as a meat substitute that was not rationed. "New" fish emerged. Max was far ahead of others in our area with fresh tuna fish, with red meat that actually looked like beef. In those days, everyone cooked tuna to a fare-thee-well, very well done and gray throughout - not like nowadays, when it is served mostly rare, and even eaten raw in sushi.

The second revolution was the post-WWII arrival of frozen food, which included fish. People in Iowa who had never eaten ocean fish were able to get it in their frozen food case, and since it had been frozen pretty soon after it was caught, not bad at all. Fish is "fishy" and repellent when it is not fresh. Even strong flavored oily fish such as bluefish and mackerel are not "fishy" when they are fresh.

Max was in on both revolutions, and also saw Vatican II come along in 1965, when Catholics were let off the requirement of meatless Fridays, but by then the whole country had gotten used to fish. And during all of it, in Max's store, you didn't have to worry. You were safe because Max's reputation was well earned; the standards were very high.

Fish such as haddock or mackerel are pretty sad the third or fourth day in a retail situation. They lose their vibrancy, their freshness. Their clear eyes become cloudy.

My friend Dave Scher, seeking precise answer in all things, once asked me, "when does the fish lose its freshness, at 36 hours, 41 hours, 73 hours?" the answer is, it's an art, not a science. You just know if you have experience. There are lots of variables: mackerel delivered in a barrel of seawater and ice, which is the way we used to get it, will last an extra day or two if it's in the barrel instead of lying out on ice in the case. It'll last longer if it nestles into the ice rather than lying on top of it. Better yet if the ice comes up and over the fish.

We would see Max throw 50 or 100 pounds of fish out the back door (or tell one of us to do it) when he didn't like the way it looked. This was not rare; it would happen a few times each year. Garbage men took it away.

Max had a passion about fresh fish, but he was not a saint. So he had another outlet for fish that maybe looked like he didn't want to sell it. There were a couple of restaurant-owner friends who had an understanding with Max for him to just call when there was a chance for them to pop in and pick up a bargain. We would also cook lobsters and crabs that looked a little slow.

Since Max bought fish almost every day from the overnight fishermen who came into Boston each morning, even on the second or third day, Max's fish would be better than the restaurant owner could buy elsewhere. In those days, and even today, it wasn't that hard to beat the chain stores who were dependent on central buying and distribution which added time, at least a day or two and more, before the fish reached the local store. Nowadays, that's eased up: a store manager, say on Cape Cod, has the authority to buy some of his or her fish from local suppliers.

Which brings us to a little drama that was acted out many times in the store, at least a dozen times witnessed by me, with identical dialogue each time, like Kabuki theatre.

Every so often, a woman who had not been in the store would drift in and stand facing the fish case, the display case nearest to the front door. This was Lady #2 waiting for Max to finish with Lady #1. Max was scraping scales off a haddock for Lady #1, with his back to them. The fish cutting board was a heavy plank about a foot wide, about six feet long, and almost two inches thick. It straddled the sink and was about half the width of the sink, so you could cut fish and just shove the pieces you cut off into the sink.

Now Max was rinsing off the fish with the cold-water hose. Finally, Max snaps a piece of the butcher paper off the big roll with the cutter, wraps the fish, bags it, rings up the sale and Lady #1 leaves.

Max says, "Yes, ma'am?"

The innocent Lady #2 says, pointing at a haddock resting on the ice in the case "Is it fresh?"

Uh-oh.

Max says, "No." The woman is stunned.

"W-what do you mean, no?" Max settles into a Talmudic role, which can be compared to the Socratic method of asking questions to arrive at a philosophy.

He says, genially, "Why did you come here to shop?"

"My friends in Chelsea were all raving about your fish."

"Well, okay, if I was the kind of man who had bad fish and you asked me if it was fresh, I would say, 'yes' wouldn't I?"

Lady #2 is reeling a little bit and finally says, "Could I have the haddock in the middle, please?"

SATURDAY: David

January 29, 1938 was bitterly cold, and in downtown Everett at 4:00 am, a few stores were spilling light onto the dark sidewalks. One of them was the Norwood Market. It was always an early start on Saturdays for Max Bennett and his manager Arthur Dalrymple. And they would be going till almost midnight. On this Saturday morning, he was wearing a rumpled day-before shirt. He had a fresh one he would change into about 8 am, like an actor "going on." This was just one of the many theatre-like aspects of life in this retail situation, leading years later to his sons getting writing ideas about this dramatic place and this dramatic man. My kid brother Sidney had a title for years: "The Case and the Block."

Artie was dressed for the day and wouldn't change. Also set for the day was the eternal cigarette dangling from the corner of his mouth and sending smoke up into his eyes so he was always squinting. About 5'11" with a stolid strong body, sandy hair and deliberate movements, he was the best fish-cutter around, and taught all of Max's sons this skill. He was from Nova Scotia and so was sometimes called a "herring choker" (herring pronounced heron), one of those stereotyping names.

Friday was fish day, so the front glass case and the front window display area, which was really a sloping tiled sink, were washed down with soap and water after the store closed at 6pm. Then vanilla diluted in water was used as a deodorant. Now the store was ready for meat day.

Saturday was a marathon day, busy from 4:30am to almost midnight. Max and his manager arrived together in the dark on this Saturday morning, and first thing, while the window area was still empty, Dalrymple taped up two or three poster-paint price signs to the front window, "RIB ROAST 15c/lb." and "HAMBURG 2lbs for 25c."

The only other stores up this early on Norwood Street were Young's Bakery, with its heavenly confections, two doors away nearer to the square, and on the corner in the other direction, Pal's Luncheonette, the only one actually open to customers.

The Norwood Market was a sanctuary of warmth for Max and Artie, with containers of coffee and doughnuts from Pal's sitting on the cutting bench in the back room. Then they buttoned up long white coats and tied on aprons over the coats.

Then they started on some of the big jobs. One by one, Max carried whole chucks, already boned, rolled, and tied, out of the cooler and onto the cutting bench, a 2"x3'x6' wooden block. The 16"x24"x24" butcher block was reserved for use with a cleaver.

Then he divided the long cylinders into four or five chuck pot roasts, and covered each one with butcher wrapping paper that he folded in on itself in a sort of crude origami, leaving the face of the roast to show off the more attractive end of the cut.

At the same time, Artie cut some oven roasts: boneless rump roasts, top sirloin roasts, bottom of the round roasts, and top of the round roasts.

Artie then started on icing the front window and the front case.

There were bushels of cracked ice that had been delivered and left outside the back door alongside a delivery by L&K Trucking of a dozen boxes of iced chickens. Artie brought in the thin-slatted wire-bound boxes of poultry and was busy chopping off chicken heads and feet. Heads into the garbage, feet saved. Most people don't know that chicken feet are a delicacy, but there was always a minority that asked for them. Now you can only find them in Chinatown poultry shops.

The chicken boxes and its ice were thrown out. Artie used only fresh ice in the displays that were being set up. Anyone who came in early helped carry the round-bottomed bushel baskets of ice and the chickens out to the front display case and the front window display area. Artie displayed the chickens with the legs bent and the wing tips tucked under the wings.

Also in the window today was corned beef, made in the store, and the specials of the day: smoked shoulders and the big seven-rib standing rib roasts.

Max had bought a lot of seven-rib standing rib roasts.

Arriving at 4:30am were Eddie Walsh, another of Max's full-timers, and my brother Joey, the Harvard man. Two of my heroes.

Joey would start breaking down a big leg of veal from the Rath Packing Company of Waterloo, Iowa, so he could cut veal cutlets, and Eddie would bring pork loins out of the cooler and start on pork chops.

Eddie was a classic handsome New England Irish Catholic and a great tenor besides. He had blue eyes and sharp features and tightly waved sandy hair. He was very reminiscent of Dick Powell, the movie star. He would break into song during the day on a busy Saturday and charm everybody, especially the women.

Joey was another one of these handsome devils. I never looked at Fred MacMurray without thinking of Joey. I never looked at Dick Powell without thinking of Eddie, and I never looked at Spencer Tracy without thinking of my father.

I was 11 and I had an innocent view of the reaction to these men from the women who came into the store. My word for it was "gaga". A lot of the women were "gaga" all over these guys. When my sister, three years younger than Joey, had a high school group of girls come to the house to study, I saw the reaction when Joey would walk down the hall past their door. They would roll their eyes and slump onto their books. They were "gaga" all over. One of those girls married him many years later. I didn't really know what "gaga" meant. It was just my way of describing this silly foolish stuff.

I arrived about 7:30am with the rest of the "help". Renahan and Shea, MDC cops who worked part-time for Max. My mother Lillian's brothers, the terribly sweet and good-natured little uncles Frankie and Henry, who worked occasionally for Max, were only a little taller than Lillian at five foot three. Slim Renahan and fat Shea were a sort of Laurel and Hardy. Renahan's most memorable characteristic was when he was cutting something and his glasses slipped down his nose, he would put the tip of the knife into the nosepiece and push the glasses up. You couldn't watch this without holding your breath.

By 7:30, Joey would have been cutting thin veal cutlets for a couple of hours and then started on thin slices of beef bottom of the round for bracciolla, for our large number of Italian customers. These jobs I inherited a few years later.

In the front case and in the window, on ice, were rib roasts, legs of lamb, shoulder of lamb, chickens, chuck pot roasts, bottom of the round oven roasts, corned beef, shin bones, lamb breasts and veal breasts.

There were also reminders of Friday. The window might hold a display of cooked lobsters, and in the front case, the big shiny gallon cans of shelled oysters and shelled clams, sold in pint and half-pint containers

In the middle case were steaks and chops: three trays of Max's boneless rib-eye steaks, top of the round steak, rump steak, boneless sirloin, T-bone, and porterhouse. There were three trays of pork chops, plus lamb rib chops and lamb kidney chops, now called loin chops, lamb shoulder steaks, beef kidneys attached to their suet, beef liver, calves liver.

All the items in the delicatessen case, nearest the back room, had to be refreshed: a big deep tray of sausage meat, made only by Max from pork roast, pork chop fat trimmings, and spices. It could not have been more fatty and could not have been more popular (it almost always sold out). There were frankfurters, salamis, baloneys, boiled ham, whole hams, half hams and slices with the little round bone in, olive loaf, ham hocks, a wooden tub of mincemeat mix during the holidays, head cheese, and whole fresh beef tongues arranged in two rows of four, pointed ends facing the customers, a weird sight.

Max was never too busy to stop if there were some six or eight year old kid staring at the tongues and say, "do you know what that is?"

The kid would shake his head side to side, "No."

"It's a cow's tongue." Pause. "Do you know something about that cow's tongue?"

The kid shakes his head again, "No".

Max drives it home: "It never told a lie."

Before opening the double front doors at 8am, Artie said, "Davey, sawdust." I got one of the big burlap bags of sawdust out of the back room, dragged it half way down the customer side of the store, cut it open and dumped about two-thirds of it on the floor. Then I tied up the bag, put it away and brought out the iron rake. It was an easy fun job to spread the sawdust throughout the store with the rake, mostly on the customer side of the glass cases. It gave the store an inviting old-fashioned look, which was obviously one of Max's ideas.

You would be delighted at eleven years old to be told by Dalrymple, "Davey, get the sawdust." Even in those days people liked the sawdust look, and Max knew it.

Saturday was a long busy flurry of brown Kraft paper bags being filled and handed over to customers, after they paid their bill at the cashier's booth at the far end of the store. Coffee containers, the big parallel-sided cylindrical pint "cans" that we used for the shelled oysters, sat on shelves and cutting tables all over the store.

Meal breaks were catch-as-catch-can, mostly taken at Pal's Luncheonette up Norwood Street. You could take a steak from the store up to Pal's and for a dollar they would cook it and give you a whole meal to go with it.

Saturday often ended around midnight at our house with Max, Dalrymple, and two or three of the "help", along with lots of food and open bottles of Canadian Club and Four Roses on the kitchen table. It was noisy and argumentative and joyous, all of the men relieved that the long day was over, and a bit over the top after the first big belt of whiskey. Also relieved was my mother, especially if she had been in the cashier's booth all day, even if she had left the store a few hours earlier than the others, when clean up began, to get the food ready.

In a way, the most interesting thing about Saturday, the Jewish Sabbath, was that Max was the President of the synagogue, and ran a mainstream food market full of pork chops and lobsters, way beyond the Jewish dietary food laws.

When customers started arriving on this day, there was a fairly brisk business, with the out-front men bringing chickens into the back room to be cleaned out whole or cut up.

"Would you like your chicken whole or cut up, ma'am?" "Yes, please."

There were also customers having stew beef ground up into hamburg. "Ground just once, please."

Once in a while one of the back room guys would fill a request for a crown roast made from a loin of pork, or to take the bone out of a leg of lamb, and maybe tie it up.

A lot of pork shoulders were going out the door in the brown paper bags, but a funny thing was happening. Ten o'clock, ten-thirty, eleven o'clock, and no rib roasts were selling. It became a topic of conversation.

First, the guys were asking each other, "Hey what's with the rib roasts?" Then Artie, genuinely caring, but also always happy to deliver a zing to Max, asked Max, "Hey, what's with the rib roasts?"

Max's stare said he had been thinking about it, and he didn't need any help thinking about it more.

A couple of minutes later, he called me over, "David." "Go to the other stores and check the price of rib roast that they're getting." Okay. I took a small yellow pencil from the cashier and folded up some wrapping paper and shoved it in my pocket.

Right out the front door, I could see the Enterprise across the street had a sign in the window just like ours, "Beef Rib Roast 15c/lb." Also across the street was the Woburn Provision Company. I went inside and saw rib roast marked 15c/lb. Then I left Norwood Street and went out into Everett Square with quite a few more stores: the First National, the A&P, Stop and Shop, McKinnon's Market, and Everett Public Market.

Everywhere was the same 15c/lb. I didn't need my pencil and paper. Then I climbed the hill up Broadway past the high school where my classmate Bob Ericson's family had a market on Hancock Street.

I went inside. Rib Roast 15c/lb. I hurried back to the store and told Max, "Pa, everybody has the same price, 15 cents a pound, same as us." A couple of the guys heard me and in ten seconds everyone in the store knew, and started buzzing. "How much will Max cut the price? How much can you cut it when it's only 15 cents a pound?"

"What do you suppose he paid wholesale?"

Max looked like he was thinking, but he didn't take too long. He called Artie into the back room and they were rummaging around old posters and taped a new price over the price on the poster.

Then we could all see: the new price was 25c/lb! Max had made our price the highest price in town!

We almost sold out. There were a few lonely standing ribs in the window and a couple in the cooler.

Decades later, I told this story to my friend Art Widder, who teaches business courses in Portland, Oregon, and he told me about stories commonly studied in which big companies saved whole divisions by raising the price on a product that wasn't moving, especially jewelry.

The memory of the rib roast story came to me when I was in advertising years later, too, when I observed that the most expensive product in every category sold like hotcakes: Mercedes, Rolex, Norelco shavers, Braun coffee makers, all had trouble keeping up with demand.

It's a simple principle. Perception is stronger than reality, or, as Art Widder said, perception IS reality. The highest priced item in each class must be the best, right?

This was understandable for business professors and advertising men to see this, but not bad for an American immigrant retailer to grasp in 1938.

But what was Max doing open on Saturday anyway? Saturday was the Jewish Sabbath, and he was President of the Synagogue! I wish I had asked him, but I never did, neither Sid nor I did, and I can't imagine Joey doing it, but I can imagine the irreverent and flamboyant Sylvia throwing it at him, as much as she loved him. It wasn't a question of fear; we could say anything to him, and did all the time. It was more a question of it being a little uncomfortable to ask. And I don't think anyone at the synagogue asked either. Lots of Jews worked on Saturdays in this wonderful bountiful country, but none of them were President of the Synagogue. We satisfied ourselves, that is, Sylvia, Sid, and I, with one conversation in which we smugly labeled him "hypocrite", which was much too strong, and never spoke of it again. And me with the lingering feeling that we were wrong to even think it. I also wish I had asked Joey or my mother. Probably my inhibition there was an unarticulated feeling that it might hurt her feelings.

Sid's opinion now is that Max would have said, "That's business," meaning that it was separate from the rest of your life.

Along the same lines, I would guess that Max would say that whatever you had to do to make a living, or to survive was justified. There is a deep foundation for this thought. In the Talmud, Jews are given permission, when necessary to save their lives, to declare allegiance to another religion, as many did in the Spanish Inquisition.

Max bore all this lightly, and seemed to enjoy every aspect of it. On Sundays he was out of the house before any of us were up, just like the rest of the week, and he would find a synagogue where he could participate in a service, whether he was president there or not. He would periodically have some eruption at one of these synagogues and quit (at least once over a fight about the Hebrew language curriculum in the Hebrew school adjunct of the temple), and go become president of another synagogue. Because many Jews worked on Saturdays, the Jewish Sabbath, the services on Sunday were a little more elaborate, a little lengthier, with a heavier attendance than was justified by what amounted to the first weekday of the Jewish week.

In Everett, with a population of maybe a hundred families, there were three synagogues; the Malden Street Shul, the Irving Street Shul, and the Community Center. In order to worship, Jews need ten men to make up a minyan, without a Rabbi. Max once said, to explain the argumentative qualities of Jews, that if you had a town with 30 men, you would have three synagogues. This also helps to make Israel a little less puzzling. There is a saying, "If you have two Jews, you will have four opinions."

Hebrew houses of worship are mostly divided into Orthodox, Conservative and Reform. (There is what's called Reconstructionist.) I think you could attend any of the synagogues in Everett and consider yourself Orthodox or Conservative, depending on your lifestyle. If you kept a Kosher home, you were Orthodox. If you were a little less strict, you were Conservative. Reform was something they had in Boston and Newton, were rich people had services in English and might not even wear yarmulkes.

On these Sundays, Max would arrive home from his satisfying service loaded with heavenly food. He would have three big Kraft paper bags, and a torrent of wonderful things would appear. Bulkies (pronounced boolkies), a hard and crispy outside, white inside roll. There were also the softer braided rolls, eggy-yellow inside and egg-white-shellacked outside, lox (smoked salmon), whole salt herrings and herring in cream sauce, whole small whitefish with their leathery oily skins, whitefish spread, velvety smoked fishes sturgeon and sable, bagels, Jewish rye bread, pumpernickel, butter, cream cheese, Babka, cheese Danish and raspberry Danish of a quality that I don't think you can find anymore, and doughnuts that you certainly cannot find anymore, old traditional New England fried doughnut, both jelly-filled and ring-shaped.

Although we ate meals together as a family a reasonable amount of time, Sunday morning, with its informality and Sunday papers and food, was the happiest one for me. It was all from the Jewish delicatessen and bakery neighborhood in Revere. Brother Sid and I wondered how he did this in the years when he had no car.

We would not have been up long and not yet dressed when he got back but we were a match for his shopping. The Sunday Boston Globe would soon be all in pieces and spread all over the place and we would all be carrying food with and without plates all over the place, and reading parts of the paper. I remember how important the "funnies" were when I was young: Mutt and Jeff, Blondie, Maggie and Jiggs, and the Katzenjammer Kids. Very important.

When I was dressed, I walked to Shapiro's drug store and picked up Max's Sunday New York Times. He would read it for several hours on Sunday, and for the following several nights. He had taught himself to read and write English, and seemed to read with ease, but his handwriting was another matter. It was awful but just legible. Max also read the Bible and the Talmud, and an occasional novel like *The Apostle* by Sholom Asch.

In the synagogue, I know he had the respect as "a learned man" and I know he loved the endless analytical arguments about the day's text, which followed the services. He had attended the Yeshiva in Vilna his last year in Lithuania, and it obviously gave him a good grounding in the Torah that he never lost. He was witty and funny in his own right, but he never became skilled enough in English to stay out of trouble in his writing. It's riddled with misspellings. But all that is understandable and we're thankful for what we have.

He would slip into a malapropism every so often, and I think we were too polite to correct him. Not just that, but they were so full of truth, it wouldn't hit you for a few seconds that he had created a new version of an old phrase. One was, I think to get someone to go along with an eating-out proposal, "Don't be an cold blanket." Another one, commenting on some character in the news, "I think there's a motto to his madness." If the radio were too loud, he would say, "Make the radio slower."

To me, these were priceless.

FINDING LILLIAN: Sid

Compared to the amount of information we have about Max, we know very little of Ma's history before she came to America. It is only recently, for instance, that we found out that the family name in Shepetivka, Ukraine was Kosakowsky, not Kaplan.

She was born December 15 1895, to Anna and Peissech Kosakowsky. Her Hebrew name was Rachel Leah.

Peissech Kosakowsky is listed on the manifest for the ship Zaandam out of Rotterdam to New York arriving January 13 1896. Birth date about 1868. Age 28.

Paul Kaplan appears in the United States 1900 census as a single boarder in Newburyport, Massachusetts. Born July 1868. Age 31. Married for 7 years. Russian. Occupation - rag sorter.

Lillie Kaplan (Lillian Ruth), 15, appears in the 1910 census as the daughter of Paul and Annie. She has a sister Dora (Dorothy), 2. Paul's occupation is Junk Dealer. They are living in Chelsea, Massachusetts.

The 1920 Census shows the addition of two sons: Francis (Frank), 9, and Henry, 1.

Since we were told that Ma came to America when she was four years old, we can assume that she and Anna came here sometime in 1900 between the June 1900 Census and December 15. Perhaps someday the NARA will reveal its secrets and we will find a ship manifest with their names.

So it looks like soon after Lillian was born, Paul goes to America, works in the rag business to save enough money to bring his family here, starts his own junk dealership, increases his family, and is living the American Dream.

Ma grew up in Chelsea and graduated Chelsea High School June 24, 1913. Before she graduated she was already working in a high-rise office building in Boston as a bookkeeper. How many immigrant children accomplished that in 1913?

One of my earliest memories is a feeling of pride when the ladies of Ma's eight-member bridge club would leave the house complaining that Lillian was always winning.

I'm sure it was her intelligence that attracted Max. A mutual friend introduced them, and Max was smart enough to make her his bride as much as Lillian was smart enough to choose him as her husband. They were married January 30, 1917.

She was Max's partner. They loved and respected each other. Ma took care of the home that Max provided for. When needed, she was also the cashier in the store. Their conversations were long and intimate, mostly in Yiddish. I'm sure now that it was deliberate. They did not want us knowing what their financial problems were, and later, the things that were going on during the war.

I suppose that because she was a big sister to three siblings, she got some practice in child rearing. Most of my memories are hazy: cooking in the kitchen, kissing me goodnight, taking me to Chelsea to visit Aunt Dolly, taking me to the Esplanade concerts in Boston. I know she was always there for me.

One memory I do not have is when I was eleven months old. I was told I had diphtheria and almost died. The tracheotomy they did on me was an experiment - instead of leaving the hole open to heal, they sewed it up - perhaps allowing me to have an ordinary voice. But that is not the important part of the story.

After they took me home, my siblings were told not to touch me because Ma believed I was too frail.

Evidently, when I was about five years old, someone accidently knocked me down - and I didn't die. So the gloves were off and I suffered from having been the spoiled brat that I was.

I've often wondered what all those punches and tears would have done to me had I not had my understanding mother.

Through my sicknesses, cuts, bruises, good marks, stupidity, laughter, disobeying, compliments, tears, and stubbornness, I got hugs and love and incredible security.

EVERETT: David

If you're driving south from Maine on Route 1, you'll do a little bit of New Hampshire, and then enter Massachusetts. Going through Maine and New Hampshire, and for a few miles in Massachusetts, you'll know where you are.

That is, the towns are separate, distinct. But after just a short time in the Bay State, forget it. And by the time you get down around Danvers and Peabody, you are into the Boston suburb maelstrom, a mess in which you are never sure where you are, where one irregularly-shaped town runs into the next and where there is a very little in the way of signs.

People still live their entire lives in a suburb of Boston and have a very difficult time once they need to leave it to try to find another suburb. Nowadays public transit and the highways help, but it's still hard except for some people who are gifted with aptitudes that make this nightmare simple. They are the Boston savants.

At Saugus, if you switch to Route 99 (formerly Route 1), it will take you through Everett, my hometown and where I lived an idyllic and happy life until age 18, when I went off to World War II.

Route 99 becomes Broadway in Everett, and from Glendale Square rises dramatically, up a big hill, and just over the crown is the Parlin Junior High School on the left and the old Everett High School on the right; then the hill goes down to Everett Square. If you are walking, a right turn off Broadway in Everett Square would bring you into Norwood Street, which had a variety of about a dozen shops including my father's meat and fish store called the Norwood Market. If you are driving, Norwood Street is one-way into Everett Square.

Norwood Street, the center of the family's attention for 20 years, augmented and duplicated the larger group of stores along Broadway, and competed with them.

For the three years of Everett High, I walked to the store after school, which let out at 1:30. I would go down Broadway from the High School, past the Capitol movie theater, past a few stores and a few residences and the old City Hall. Between Court Street and Norwood Street, there was a church, a bank, and Kresge's 5-and-10-cent store. Kresge's was on the corner of Norwood Street, and there was a doughnut machine in Kresge's window.

From a big conical contraption at the top of the machine, it extruded moist dough in the shape of a doughnut, which dropped into the perimeter of a big round tub of hot fat, and was gently moved in a circle to make room for the next doughnut. In the outer circle, the doughnuts were fried on the bottom, and halfway around, a paddle turned each doughnut over so the other side could fry. The machine had a dozen doughnuts going all the time, and at the end of the cycle, the fried doughnut was turned out onto a metal slide to a trough, where someone had to pick them up and box them. I was never in too much of a hurry to be able to stop and watch the doughnuts.

They were delicious old New England doughnuts, great whether plain or covered with granulated sugar.

I would turn into Norwood Street and pick up some parts of a lunch, walk into my father's store, and be working by about 2pm, waiting on customers out front or cutting meat in the back room.

Most days I stopped for a chocolate or vanilla milk shake (no ice cream) or a frappe (with ice cream) at Giaccobbe's Drug Store on the corner, and

a hard roll at the heavenly Young's Bakery a couple doors from our store closer to Everett Square. You can't get a roll like that anymore. The outside was so crisp it broke like glass when you bit into it, and it had a snow-white, substantial interior.

In the back room of the store, where we had a stove to cook lobsters and corned beef, I would fry a small steak, usually a slice of tenderloin, or else a rib-eye, and make a sandwich out of it and the crusty roll.

For years that was my walk after school.

If you stay on 99, you'll go through some more anonymous towns and into Boston. In Everett, in the thirties, you'd pass a huge yellow mound of sulphur, 20 or 30 feet high, that would sting your nostrils from a quarter of a mile away, that belonged to the Monsanto Chemical Company. Also, in 1938, just before the sulphur, you'd see Everett Station, the end of one arm of the octopus-like elevated subway system that would take you into Boston if you weren't driving.

Now that station is gone.

There was a rearrangement of the transit system in 1975, and I think it struck a mortal blow at Everett. They changed the direction from Boston of the elevated subway one stop earlier at Sullivan Square, where the Schrafft's Chocolate factory in Charlestown was. The elevated continued to Malden. You could still get to Everett, but you had to take a bus from Sullivan Square.

It made Everett less convenient, and I believe it altered the economy and future of Everett through to the present day.

Everett was a bustling, hustling town in the old days, even in the Depression, and the pile of sulphur was a symbol of the local economy. It meant industry and jobs.

Another symbol was the General Electric plant, which employed a few hundred in the Thirties and thousands as World War II approached. There was also a wholesale and manufacturing section of Everett, and still is, and during the Thirties it made Everett a peculiarly healthy place economically. The stores in Everett Square were busy, too, and drew people from other towns, not just from Everett.

The candy bar "Charleston Chew" was made in Everett, and all my life, when I bought one, I would look for the "Everett, Mass." on the label. Now they are made in Cambridge, Massachusetts

The suburbs of Boston are all different from each other, even though they are almost indistinguishable geographically.

There are rich towns and poor towns, and almost purely residential towns, but none with the character that Everett had in the Thirties.

Of course there were people in Everett suffering from the hard times, and I knew some in High School, but generally I was sheltered from the Depression, and I believe Everett was, too.

I never heard the word "Depression" when I was growing up in Everett in the 1930's. My mother didn't confront me when I woke up, and say, "Honey, the country is experiencing a Depression. Please keep that in mind as you go to your fifth-grade classroom today."

There never was any discussion in the house about whatever problems the Depression was bringing to the country or to the family. That may have just been part of the fact that no bad news of any kind was ever discussed in English in front of the children, anyway. We were sheltered.

So my impression looking back is that there was no Depression. I was sheltered from it in other ways, too.

First of all, Max owned a food store: meat, fish, fruits, vegetables, and some dairy products.

I would say we were middle class, but if you are going to be in a middle-class family in a Depression, my advice is pick one with a food store.

There is always plenty to eat.

We had a lot of fish, and it was great. Max sold the freshest fish you could imagine, and Lillian was, within a limited repertoire, a great cook. There was haddock, there was cod, halibut, mackerel, all fried in the custom of the times, but never greasy. She was a wizard with smelts. I never had them as perfect as she made them ever again.

The greatest thing she made was next-day fish salad. This was usually made with the leftover flaky white fishes, Cain's Mayonnaise, and always with chopped celery, a hallmark of New England fish salads.

Most things in the store were done in cash, except for the checks Max had to write to companies like the Rath Packing Company and Armour and Company. So I saw a lot of cash. It looked unlimited to me, come to think of it.

When I was 15 and graduated to meat-cutter from order-boy in the store, Max, who paid me (and my brothers) as if we were outsiders, gave me fifty dollars a week, which was a lot of money in those days for a teenager or even for a grown-up.

And unlike all my friends, who had to contribute some of their earnings at home, I didn't have to. Donny Bookman, my best friend, made about fifteen dollars a week at a couple of part-time jobs, and had to cough up ten of it at home towards "room and board."

Max and Lillian were generous, but I think now that Charlie and Ida Bookman were doing a better job of putting their sons into touch with reality.

But thinking back again, the biggest way the Depression was hidden from me was the atmosphere of my hometown, Everett.

Everett Square and the store were always hustling and bustling, especially on Fridays and Saturdays. My thought, looking back, is that Everett was actually excused somehow from the Depression.

Anyway, I was unconscious of it, and unaware generally about politics and the economy for many years. I was just living a happy and even idyllic life until age 18, when I went off to World War II. I loved school, I loved the store, and I loved the family life. There was always something going on.

Everett was, and is, a completely built-up town (no empty lots) about two miles by two miles, with a population of about 50,000 before WWII, and about two-thirds of that now. Everett was 80% or 90% Italian-Catholic and Irish-Catholic with the corresponding big families, and the corresponding Italian-Catholic church and the Irish-Catholic church. In the 1930's, an Italian-American boy dating an Irish-American girl caused a fuss among the families that reminded you of the Montague's and Capulet's.

Now, according to John Hanlon, Everett City Clerk in 2002, Everett is a "bedroom community" for people who work in Boston and elsewhere. That means one or two people are occupying a house or apartment that once held many more. And Everett has its share of the many ethnic groups that have moved into Boston and suburbs. But Everett, uniquely in the area, also has a lot of industry, which differentiates it from other bedroom communities. In fact, it was once known as "The City of Industrial Diversity."

This gave Everett the health, which I believe I saw as a boy, but didn't really understand, or even think about, until I revisited that era for this book.

In 1944, my High School class numbered 661. In 2002, the graduating class numbered 435. The population had declined from 50,000 to 35,000. But Everett was completely occupied. There was no place to build, unless you knocked down a few houses to put up an apartment house. Everett, to all appearances booming during the Depression, and depressing during the boom and bust of the 90's and 2000's, finally seemed to bottom out in the 90's.

Norwood Street, which I always visited when I was in the area, because of my strong sentimental attachment to it, had become rundown and tacky by the late 1980's, but was unmistakably making a sharp comeback in 2002.

On the corner, which used to be Kresge's 5&10, was a smart new restaurant. Giaccobbe's Drug Store on the opposite corner had long since become a Brigham's, the once-legendary ice-cream parlor chain.

In the Thirties, Everett's football team was known nationally. There was a nice diversity, which in those days meant there were Irish Catholics, Italian Catholics, Protestants and Jews. I had all kinds of friends, and as a teenager, would go to midnight Mass on Saturday nights with Catholic friends, which excused them from having to go to church on Sunday.

So that was my routine for three years, walking a triangle from home to school (about a mile) to the store (a quarter mile) to home (a mile) five days a week.

On Saturday, it was just home to store to home.

ZORACH: Sid

David should have told this story.

Rabbi Liftman came to the house on Main Street to be the Moyel for David's Briss (circumcision ceremony). He is perfect for the part. He has the black clothes and the grey beard. He has a reputation as a Biblical scholar.

Everyone is there. It is 1926 and everything is onwards and upwards. The store is doing very well, Max is buying triple-deckers, and they own a Pierce Arrow car.

At the proper moment, Rabbi Liftman asks Max the new baby's name.

Max says, "Zorach".

The Rabbi questions, "Zorach?"

Max says, "Zorach. It was my mother's father's name."

The Rabbi says, "What kind of name is that? I never heard it. It's not in the Bible."

Max is livid. Does anyone think he doesn't know his grandfather's name? Does anyone think he doesn't know his Bible? The argument goes on for a few minutes.

Finally, Max says, without consulting anyone, especially Lillian, "All right. His name is David".

So Zorach became David.

*****

Four years later, it is time for my Briss.

Again, everyone is there. However, it is 1930 and things are not so good. The Pierce Arrow is gone. Max's customers owe him money. His tenants owe him rent and food money. It will not be long before the store and the triple-deckers will be gone.

Max is in no mood to be crossed.

Rabbi Liftman comes and finally asks, "What is the baby's name?"

Max says, "Zorach".

The Rabbi says, "Didn't we already do this? It's not a Biblical name!"

Max says, "Oh, yes it is". And he produces a Bible.

He has the passage bookmarked, and without a word, he points to it.

There is no more discussion.

Who is the Biblical scholar now?

I became Zorach. Somehow, Zorach became Sidney, for which I am very grateful.

Note: Zorach can be found in Genesis, Chapter 38. The story tells how Zorach and Pharez were twins whose mother had them by her father-in-law.

LILLIAN: David

Two of my most vivid memories of my mother are in my mind as black-and-white movie scenes, oddly alike with cross-lighting and dramatic shadows.

One is when she brought Sidney home from the hospital a few days after he was born. I was four years old in 1930. We lived on Main Street in Everett, in the second-floor flat of a triple-decker near Max's store.

Max didn't own a car at that time, and the neighborhood barber named Duca, who was a friend, had driven Max in his Pierce Arrow to pick up Lillian and Sidney from the Malden Hospital in Malden.

In a move that seems terribly modern to me now, she had Max carry the baby. I was standing back against the wall on the second floor landing in the shadows. She came directly at me and hugged and kissed me, and thereby eased the territorial invasion by the sibling. Max and the baby were out of focus in the background.

I didn't know what I had been feeling, but I felt better then.

*****

I was 12 in the sixth grade and my best friend was Wilbur Heywood. My parents knew him and his parents knew me. We were exemplary boys, polite and neat and getting good grades.

Now the sixth grade was having a Saturday outing. There would be buses and it was a trip out to the "country" where there would be a picnic and games.

I was told I could go if Wilbur was getting permission to go. Wilbur told me he couldn't go.

Apparently I lost my sanity temporarily. There was a girl in our class named Norma Shuman, a dark beauty with big almond-shaped eyes. She was going and that's why I wanted to go. I was unbelievably innocent and didn't have a coherent idea of why I wanted to go, but there it was.

So I told my mother that Wilbur had permission and I went.

I remember having a happy day, consisting mostly of chasing Norma over the grassy meadows, and once, stumbling, knocking her down. We laughed a lot. Late in the afternoon, the bus dropped us at the school parking lot and I walked home.

As I climbed the stairs to the second-floor flat on Vine Street, the lighting was reversed from when they brought Sidney home.

Instead of me in the shadows, my mother was. She was way back on the landing in the dark, with a bit of light angling across her face. She looked like a silent-movie actress, expressing a lot of pain mostly through the eyes.

"Mrs. Heywood called," she said evenly, but certainly cooler than she had ever spoken to me. "She said that since you and Wilbur didn't get to go today, the Heywoods wanted to make up for it by taking you both on a family picnic tomorrow."

Her face conveyed the awful knowledge that she had told Mrs. Heywood that I lied. She never mentioned this again, and there was no punishment.

There was pure instinctive genius.

It had ten times the effect of punishment, which would have given me some relief. It influenced the rest of my life… I was unable to lie, and I got into a lot of trouble for that reason.

I never had anything to do with Norma again, except some furtive hellos and a breezy friendship in school.

After a few feeble attempts at keeping the relationship with Wilbur going, the friendship was destroyed. I think he was as shocked as my mother at what I had done.

Harvard: David

HARVARD BACKS DOWN FOR MAX

THE TIME MAX WENT UP AGAINST HARVARD

MAX 2, HARVARD 0

Max had to go to see the Harvard Brahmins twice, and it wasn't Joey's fault either time.

Once it was the playboy. Max and Lillian had received a note suggesting that they take their son out of school because of his behavior outside of school.

It turned out to be a playboy with a similar name. Max had to go all the way into Cambridge to find the mistake and get it corrected. Those were not the days when you picked up the phone.

The other time was over the payments to Harvard. The payment was $100 a month and one time Max was late. A letter showed up immediately, telling him the charge for being late was $10 dollars a month and now he owed $110.00.

Max went in to Harvard and saw the man who wrote the letter.

He pointed out that Harvard was charging 120% interest a year and that seemed strange. What he was saying was that it was usurious, and the man caught the meaning.

He dropped the $10 charge.

A later Harvard story happened after the war when Joe and Bernice came back from a Harvard-Yale football game.

"Who won?" asked Max.

"Yale," said Joe.

"Ach, in drerd mein gelt!" said Max, which in English means, "My money has gone to hell!"

SYLVIA: David

For some reason, probably because we were the more adventurous of the four children, and despite the difference of six years in age, Sylvia and I teamed up a lot. I was going to say because we were the two flamboyant children, but the truth is that I was learning flamboyance from Sylvia.

The basic joke about Jewish cooking in those days was that when the roasted chicken in the platter hit the table, all the meat falls off the bones. One day having been out pushing the outer edges of assimilation, Sylvia and I had discovered rare steak in a restaurant, ordered by a friend, and we came home and excitedly told Lillian about the wonders of not overcooking meat.

We demonstrated immediately with a rib eye, of which there was always a stack in the refrigerator.

Lillian was wonderful. She laughed with delight at the eggs teaching the chickens, as Max would say, and embraced this bit of knowledge, always eager to learn something new. Especially something brought home by her fabulous children.

Another time, we brought home two cooked lobsters from a street vendor, and that was not so funny to her but she was laughing anyway at our antics. We knew damn well lobsters weren't kosher, and we were being mischievous. That didn't bother Lillian, but she drew the line. She made us spread newspapers on the porcelain sink so the lobsters didn't touch anything in the house, but she didn't stop us from eating them.

BUTTS: Sid

Cigarettes were a mystery to me when I was seven years old living on Vine Street. One day some of my buddies and I came across a pile of fairly long cigarette butts in the gutter.

We took the butts into a garage. Somebody produced some matches, and we imitated our parents by smoking.

Max smoked Herbert Tareytons and Raleighs for the coupons in each pack. Lillian smoked about once a week, in conversation with family or her friends, seated in an easy chair, holding the cigarette in her hand, palm up. This was the image that let us lovingly call her *Shanghai Lil*.

Smoking in the garage, I was coughing, smoke going up into my eyes, burning them, and burning my tongue. I toughed it out in front of everybody, but I didn't like it.

I finally went home, and took about two steps into the room when Sylvia screamed, "You've been smoking!" and started to beat my head in. She wasn't fooling. She really hurt me. She then went on about telling me to never smoke again, she would beat me - worse, she would tell Ma and Pa, and she would make me miserable.

Well. If you smoke, and it makes you cough, and it burns your eyes and your tongue, and your sister beats your head in, then even at seven years old you realize that there's not a lot to be said for smoking.

I took the hint. I never smoked again. Everybody should have a sister that will do that for you and make you forever grateful.

I have to add - Sylvia smoked.

DISCUSSIONS: Sid

Our neighbors on Baker Road in 1938 were the Atkinsons. They were a very nice couple with one son about David's age.

One day, Mrs. Atkinson and my mother were talking over the proverbial back fence between our houses. The discussion turned to families. Mrs. Atkinson said, "Oh how I envy your big family. We only have our one son, and I so wish we could have those wonderful Saturday night discussions you have."

Behind her smile, Ma was shocked and wondering if Mrs. Atkinson was pulling her leg. 'Discussions' indeed. The only thing Ma would say during those 'discussions' was "Please - be quiet" and "What will the neighbors think?" She knew how loud those 'discussions' got.

Mrs. Atkinson had always been such a respectful person that it was hard to believe that she could say anything negative about anybody.

So Ma said, "Well, it does get a little loud sometimes, I hope it doesn't bother you."

"Oh, no. I think it's wonderful," said Mrs. Atkinson.

And they went on to other things.

CANTOR: David

In 1938, we were living on Baker Road, and it was a big year. It was the year of the hurricane, and a big Chestnut tree in front of the house, about 3 feet in diameter, was partially uprooted, breaking the sidewalk. The tree leaned towards the house, but never fell on it.

Another hurricane that hit Baker Road that year was the Cantor.

Among Max's peregrinations were trips to New York and other parts of the country because he was a member of a few national organizations. There was an association of Synagogue Presidents, a Zionist group, and his lodge, the IOOF (International Order of Odd Fellows). Also there was one New York trip every year to buy two pairs of black shoes from a custom shoemaker who had saved his feet. He had had a growing problem of pain in his feet when walking and finally, happily discovered someone who could help him. It had been painful to watch him walking gingerly and a relief for everybody when he found someone to help.

Joey was to graduate Harvard and Sylvia was graduating High School next year so we were all still home.

And we were so used to Max's comings and goings we hardly noticed them.

But we all snapped to attention when he walked in one Monday in March, and, I believe without any warning to Lillian, with a man he introduced as Cantor something-or-other and that he would be staying with us.

My admiration for my mother knew no bounds. Besides loving her, I admired her extravagantly for her wit and humor and brains, and for her ever-present hard-working attack on her roles as mother, wife, nurse, comforter, cook, housekeeper, cheerleader, and money-squirreler, but I never admired her more than for her reception of the Cantor.

She was regal. Drawn up to her full five-foot-three height, with a slight, but not icy, smile, she shook hands with this invader. Max says, "I think a shul or a temple around here will want the Cantor. He is a wonderful singer. I heard him sing." And indeed he looked like a singer. About Max's height, but with a substantial paunch, he had that opera star look. Tanned and almond-eyed, with shiny black hair brushed back slickly, he looked like a heavy Al Jolson, and he was wearing a beautifully tailored suit.

The Cantor says, "I hope you don't mind. This is my diet." And he hands Lillian a piece of paper he has taken from an inside breast pocket. Invisible to the public (the Cantor) but not to me, my Mother's smile then shifted to icy. "Of course, " she says, just as any Queen of England or Boston Brahmin would.

As it turned out, it wasn't a very fancy diet. It involved things like skim milk, which we didn't have around the house, and eggs boiled instead of fried, which was not strange to us.

The Cantor altered our lives. Before he arrived, the only time we had to be quiet was on the Tuesday nights when Lillian's two-table bridge club met at Baker Road. Now we had to be quiet all the time, especially when he practiced every day. I thought he had a truly great voice. He actually was an exciting operatic tenor. He would alternately sing arias we recognized from our Enrico Caruso records and also liturgical solos we did not recognize, because he had a style we had never heard. All cantors do not sing alike.

It was suspenseful and it was fun. They brought Auntie Dolly's girl friends to him one at a time, and

I, from the stairway, looking through the bannisters at the couch in the living room, where the Cantor, not tiny, and Dolly's girlfriend, also not tiny, were struggling to find a position to kiss.

It was like an Andy Hardy film. The Baker Road dining room struck me funny, on the occasions when the whole family sat down to dinner together.

And it was accented when the Cantor was there, because we were in a slightly more formal behavior mode. So there would be polite conversation, but if you were talking to someone across the big round dining table, you had to bend to one side because a big lamp hanging from the ceiling was in your way. It was a big inverted bowl Tiffany-type lamp. In fact, I think it was a Tiffany lamp, which wouldn't have been that big a deal for the original builder of the house to manage in those days. It was the type that had a variety of fruit in the leaded glass, and very colorful. It hung from the ceiling by a chain with substantial links. In a house full of high IQ's, it never occurred to anyone to take out a few links so you wouldn't have to tilt yourself to talk to someone across the table. Certainly the link removal wouldn't have occurred to Max, who never did any work like that around the house.

We knew Max and the Cantor were visiting synagogues and temples in Boston and in various suburbs around Boston, auditioning.

For whatever reasons, he was not hired and went back to New York after a few weeks.

He didn't marry any of Dolly's girlfriends, either.

BICYCLE: David

In 1938, I was 11, in the sixth grade with the estimable teacher Miss Powers, and delivering orders for the Norwood Market on a series of used balloon-tire bicycles.

I must have owned six or eight of them over a few years, as I gradually began to wait on customers and started getting meat-cutting lessons from Eddie Walsh.

There was no formal statement about the meat-cutting lessons, but Max had obviously told Eddie to start me, and wisely stayed out of it himself.

I was buying the bikes for three or four dollars each, and was constantly repairing them and buying parts for them, mostly chains and links. I had four big wire baskets, one on each side of the front wheel and one on each side of the back wheel. They were deep and held a lot and Everett is a hilly town.

It was all uphill to the Martinsons, and Mrs. Martinson was surely the sweetest customer I ever knew. She always wanted to tip me, which I pompously refused, because I was the son of the owner of the store, and therefore could not take tips. Where did this rule come from? It was nonsense. I realized in later years that it was something I had made up.

Another delivery I liked was to the Andrews sisters, an elderly but perky pair who shared an apartment in one of Everett's few apartment buildings. Their orders were small, and they were known in the store mostly by the fact that they bought loin lamb chops (known as kidney lamb chops in those days and the most expensive thing in the store except for tenderloin) for their cat.

The Martinsons and the Andrews were in the store often, and Max's opinions on the Bible thrilled them as they chatted with him over the counter.

They were my favorites on the delivery jobs. They always seemed delighted to see me, and besides the tips, they always forced food on me, which was not much of a job for them. It was often four or five o'clock in the afternoon and they would have, besides cookies, a sandwich of a type that I never saw - little sandwiches that astoundingly had the crusts removed. And they would give me tea with a lot of milk and sugar in it.

Mrs. Martinson served up even more exotic stuff - pastries with melted cheese on them or raw fish, flavored somehow but not cooked, on crackers. This was not unfamiliar because of the smoked salmon we ate at home on Sundays.

But my most favorite delivery-cum-food was the General Electric cafeteria. In those days, there was a General Electric plant in Everett. GE had found Peter Lucas, a Greek immigrant running a tiny restaurant and invited him to create a cafeteria to offer the employees good meals at low prices. And no rent for Peter.

Peter and Max were friends and I think we were a fill-in supplier for Peter. So for several years, I delivered one or two orders a week to Peter, even after Eddie had started breaking me in on meat-cutting.

In 1941, before Pearl Harbor, there was a change. A huge factory went up almost overnight, and they built a huge cafeteria for Peter, all stainless steel and glass and brightly lighted, with a vast area of tables and chairs. And still no rent for Peter. I think he got wealthy there.

There was always a gate and a guard, but with the new plant, there was serious security. But I was just waved on through, the kid delivering food to the cafeteria.

Inside, Peter always had a big smile for me and lots of food. He was a tall, erect, dignified man, a lot like Max. Peter was the same kind of happy immigrant as my father, but a less flamboyant version.

What I remember most were the apple pie and the peach pie. Great lumpy pies, each piece of fruit cooked but distinct, and a crust you can hardly get anymore. In those days, lard was used in piecrust (I know now)and that's why it had that flavor and texture that generations of Americans miss. They wonder why their pie is not as great now as it was then. These days, there seems to be a small movement among cooks to use lard again in piecrusts.

Peter served up a standard American menu in the cafeteria, but he tried once in a while to break in the workers to some Greek dishes like moussaka and pastitsio. So Peter's was the first place I had moussaka.

These adventures in eating stimulated my palate and my interest in food that has lasted my whole life. **I had no idea about what they were building at the GE plant, and I don't remember caring.**

I remember enjoying all those deliveries, life in the store and at home, and I liked school. But not with any depth. Just a kind of hedonism, going from place to place where they fed you this great food - it all was natural, taken for granted. Empty-headed, but what else did I know?

Writing this book, I began to wonder about the GE plant. What were they making there when Peter was feeding me apple pie and milk?

I realized I had a friend high up in GE Human Resources and so I called her. I had been best man for her father, Francis Xavier Goss, a Marine who had received a battlefield commission in Korea.

She knew exactly what I should do. Call public relations at the GE Lynn plant. It turned out GE Lynn had a retired worker who came in one day a week, on Thursdays, and he was a company, or division historian.

It took weeks to connect, for different reasons.

Then I caught David Carpenter just as he and his wife returned to their house after a vacation. He didn't know anything about the cafeterias, but he knew a lot of other great stuff. The old plant was just a foundry, and they made parts for everything.

The new Lynn plant was actually owned by the Army Air Corps, and they built turbo superchargers there. It was one of the first air-conditioned buildings in America. The turbochargers went into B-17s, P-47s and P-38s

Carpenter remembered, because of the mnemonic involved, that 38 days after Pearl Harbor, the first P-38 rolled off the assembly line at Lockheed in Detroit.

In 1944, I enlisted in the Army Air Corps and was based in Biloxi, Mississippi. The first plane I flew in was a B-17. I wonder if an engine built in Everett or Lynn was on that plane.

The Everett GE plant and the factories like Lockheed's were going full-blast before Pearl Harbor, because of appropriations that FDR had gotten out of Congress.

Meanwhile, Joey was drafted in the middle of 1941, and was among the American boys who trained with broomsticks because there weren't enough rifles yet.

KOSHER: Sid

In the fall of 1939, Sylvia entered nursing school at Cambridge Hospital, which changed its name in 1947 to Mount Auburn Hospital.

A few weeks later, she was allowed to come home for a weekend. She was in tears.

The problem was that she was trying to follow the Jewish Dietary Laws, and the hospital did not have a means to help. They served creamed meat dishes. They served pork. They served cuts of meat that she knew were forbidden. She was hungry all the time.

When Max came home, he was told about the problem. In a rare move, Max took her into the living and had a talk.

Essentially, he said, "Look at you. You are learning to be a nurse. What better occupation could anybody have than to take care of people when they are sick? You are doing God's work. I know that God will forgive you completely if you have to go against some rules that men have made up. Where does it say that God made these rules? I don't want you to think about this anymore. You can eat anything. You can eat pork. You can eat bacon if that's what they serve you. So let's not worry about this anymore."

Amazing. At nine years of age when I was told of this conversation, I realized my father was making up his own rules about religion. There had been hints about this kind of thing before. There were his arguments with other Jews about the meaning of this or that. There was his attitude toward working Saturdays.

But what about those family trips to Chinese Restaurants? Did I know that pork strips were not chicken, as they tried to tell me? And what about Shrimp in Lobster Sauce?

I wondered that Sylvia didn't have her own questions and ideas. Perhaps she felt that Max being there sanctioned the Chinese meals.

I'm sure this was a beginning of a different look at my father. He was a leader. He was a freethinker. He was a rebel. He was his own man.

Of course Max had the price of the postage, but it took a World's Fair and a push from Lillian to get him to write to his brother in Israel.

In 1939, at the World's Fair in New York, Max and Lillian visited the Palestine Pavilion, where they were offering to send free postcards to anyone in Palestine. Lillian urged Max to write to his brother Nathan and he did.

None of us knew why they were not in touch, and I didn't find out why for many years, but everyone was much more taken with the postcard story at the time. It broke a long silence between the brothers, and precipitated a torrent of correspondence.

Max had always known what was going on with Nathan, through letters from Lithuania. So he knew about their father's visit to Palestine.

Ten years before Max reconnected with Nathan in Palestine in 1939; Nathan had persuaded their father Avram to come all the way from Lithuania around 1929, hoping Avram would want to settle in Palestine. But he didn't.

There were two stories connected with his visit. One story indicated he might stay. The inveterate lumberman was buying some wood and just collecting other scrap lumber, building up a supply on Nathan's farm. Max said, "He was finding lumber in Palestine, where there was no lumber."

The other story, which indicated he might not stay, was that he was unhappy about the lack of religious intensity in Nathan's family, even though they celebrated the main holidays, just like many immigrant Jewish families assimilating in America.

One reason in both countries for the diminished practice was the lack of time for it- the morning tefilin, or phylacteries, and the mincha and mairov, the before-dusk and after-dusk synagogue services.

The pioneers in Palestine and the new Americans in the United States alike threw themselves into the work they found, that they had to do, that they wanted to do, that they embraced with exuberance.

They worked with determination, such as Nathan carving a farm out of the desert, removing stone by stone, boulder by boulder from the earth, like a Vermont farmer, to get land that could be cultivated, and such as in America, Max and immigrants like him working 70-80 hours a week to make a living and a future.

Besides the work, there was an actual ideological disinterest in following the religion as assiduously as in the old country. Palestine, and later Israel, had plenty of Orthodox and Hassidim, powerful and political - way out of proportion to their numbers. But the majority of pioneers and Sabras were more relaxed about their religion. Surrounded by the actual places written about in the Bible, and thoroughly respectful of it, still they could not give it the commitment of Orthodox sects like the Hassidim and the Lubavechers.

The compromises on religion were more general than only in Nathan's family. Avram saw kibbutzim where the Jews were raising pigs. Pork is forbidden in the Dietary Laws of Orthodox Jews. In fact, the rabbinical councils in Palestine outlawed raising pigs "on the earth of Israel". They got around that by pouring huge cement pens, covering "the earth of Israel" and giving themselves another product for export, along with oranges and pecans.

Anyway, Avram didn't like the way things were and he wouldn't stay. So he went back to Lithuania, a land then and now, and throughout World War II, as anti-Semitic as any country, and we are led to

believe that the whole family was killed by Lithuanians led by Germans in 1941.

Avram Aaron Beniatovich

Paul and Hannah Kaplan

Lillian Ruth Kaplan

Chelsea High School Graduation 1913

Lillian and Max Bennett
Wedding January 30, 1917

Joseph, Sylvia, David, Sidney 1938

Lillian and Max

25th Wedding Anniversary 1942

David, Sylvia, Sidney 1942

Lillian and Max 1950

Bernice and Joseph

Irene Sylvia

David

Sid

THERE IS NOTHING WORSE: Sid

It was 1940. I was ten and in the fourth grade at the Nichols School in Everett. This was one of a few small elementary schools with grades one through four in Everett, so the fourth grade contained the oldest kids. For grades five through seven everyone went to the Hamilton School, then on to the Parlin Junior High School for grades eight and nine, and finally, to Everett High School. The exception was the Whittier School, which was then called the "trade" school for grades seven through twelve.

For some reason, I was chosen, with another boy, to deliver and bring back letters to and from the School Superintendent's office near Everett Square about a mile away. Around once a week, we were taken from class and sent on our errand.

One day, we were coming back from the office and decided to play one of our favorite games - sailing and racing pieces of wood down the street gutters. A fire hydrant had been conveniently opened so we had plenty of water. I put the letters down while we did this for a while and forgot our mission.

When we remembered what we were supposed to be doing, we went back to where I thought we put the letters, and they were gone. We searched in panic mode for a little while and couldn't find them.

We knew we had to get back, and tried to think of a story that would cover our loss. We finally fixed on the fact that a dog had come along and taken them right out of my hands.

We reported our story, got lots of quizzical looks, and were sent back to class.

About an hour later, we were summoned to the Principal's office, where a uniformed policeman and two men in suits were waiting. One of them produced the packet of letters, and held them close to me.

"Do these letters look like they have dog teeth marks on them?"

I was terrified. I said no, and quickly confessed to everything.

We were sent back to class.

When I got home, the Principal was there talking to my mother. My life was over. I was sent to my room. The Principal left and Ma said nothing to me.

Max came home. Ma told him the story, and I was sent for.

We sat at a corner of the kitchen table. Pa was very calm, but I was trembling. He spoke softly and slowly.

"I want to tell you something and I want you to listen and understand what I'm telling you. You are not a baby anymore, so you should understand.

"I want you should know that there is nothing in the world that is worse than a thief. There is nothing worse than a person who will take something that belongs to someone else. People work hard for what they've got, and a person who will steal from them is the worst person in the world.

"So you should know that there is NOTHING worse than a thief. Understand? There is NOTHING worse than a thief."

Then, very calmly, he said, "A liar is worse than a thief."

SEDERS: Sid

From the beginning, I had to ask the four questions at a Seder (the meal with a ceremony to celebrate Passover), because I was the youngest. I was the youngest until Alan, Joey's son, was old enough to ask. If Alan started when he was 6, as I did, then I was 24 when I was finally relieved of the duty.

Passover was a big holiday when I was young. Ma had to put away all our everyday dishes, utensils, and pots and pans. Then she had to get out all the dishes, utensils, and pots and pans that were used once a year for the holiday.

Then the cooking would start: Matzo balls for chicken soup, sponge cake, gefilte fish, kugel, tzimmes, and the regular chicken and beef dishes. The boxes of matzo would appear. I hated matzo. The only way I could eat matzo was if it were fried with eggs to make it soft and taste like something.

There were always lots of people at the Seders. Max presided. He did the full service, ignoring the conversations that grew up at the table. He loved this ritual as much as he enjoyed holiday services. He was the expert who had been to Yeshiva in Lithuania. He never had the problems with the rituals of religion that he did with God.

Only when participation was needed did people pay attention. The part that interested me was finding the hidden Afikamon (a matzo taken from the ritual and hidden during the Seder). If you found it, you got a wished-for prize. I usually found it, but I was banned from looking for it after I got too greedy and asked for too much when I was about 11.

In 1971 I asked Max to come to our Cape Cod home to hold a Seder for our friends. He had come to my surprise fortieth birthday party the summer before and was a big hit with the Cape Codders. He held court and was asked lots of questions - probably the ones that David and I never asked. The idea for his coming to hold a Seder had come from someone in that group.

We had gathered all the ritual food items and tried to make a Jewish meal. We got Haggadahs (books that had the text of the service) in both English and Hebrew for everyone. We had one bottle of Manischewitz sweet wine for Max, but I rebelled and got dry wines for the rest of us.

The Seder started all right (yes, I had to ask the four questions since there was no-one else), but I soon realized that everyone was paying strict attention to their books and were being very respectful of Max and the procedure. It was unnatural to me. I had never experienced a quiet Seder before. I couldn't take it, so I got up, went around the table, whispering to our guests that not only was it perfectly all right for them to talk, but I urged them to do so. The talking never rose to the level of noise I was used to, but it did help me to relax.

Max carried on disregarding everyone.

The evening was a huge success. Our friends were varied, from fishermen and carpenters to professionals, and he charmed them all. He got a huge kick out of shocking someone by telling them that the Last Supper was a Passover Seder.

MOVIES: Sid

In July 1941, for my eleventh birthday, Joe was given the day off so he could take me into Boston for two double features.

A double feature was two movies, an 'A' film with big stars that would last an hour and a half to two hours, and a 'B' movie that was a shorter western or family movie. That was not all. There were Short Subjects. There would be News (Paramount News of The World), a cartoon, (Bugs Bunny), an extra (A Pete Smith Specialty), a comedy (The Three Stooges), and a serial (Flash Gordon).

After the first double feature, we had lunch at the Essex Lunch (as David says, "now gone"). They were famous for huge hot pastrami or corned beef sandwiches, with bowls of self-serve pickles and green pickled tomatoes on the counter or tables.

Then we went to the second double feature. I don't remember the names of the movies, but I remember everything else about the day. It was a very special day because he had never done anything like that with me before.

I was with my big brother: the six-foot handsome Harvard Graduate, the family genius who entered Harvard at sixteen, and who, because he had been a geography and history major, toured the United States after graduating college - bringing me back a chunk of petrified wood from the Petrified Forest, and who knew everything, including the latest major league baseball player batting averages.

That day was a very special treat. To go into Boston, to go to the movies - twice, to go to the Essex Lunch, with my special brother, was easily memorable.

The following September, when Joe went off as a draftee to the Army, I realized why he had taken me.

He knew he would be going into the Army and wanted a special day for his kid brother to remember. I remember. I still remember.

STARTING: Sid

My first Saturday at work in the Norwood Market is memorable only because of the second Saturday.

In September 1941, at 11 years old, I walked to the store from our house on Irving Street. I was given an apron, shown how to tie it on, given a straw broom, and told to sweep up the old sawdust.

I had barely finished sweeping around a 50-gallon barrel of mackerel when Max passed by and criticized what I had done. "You're supposed to sweep up underneath the barrel, or anything else you can move."

I tried to move the barrel, but it was almost full of ice and water, so it was very heavy, as you can imagine. David took a little pity on me and tried to show me how to pull the opposite side of the barrel towards you until it was balanced on the near bottom edge of the barrel. Then you could roll it to where you wanted. If you were smart, you would first sweep the spot you wanted to place the barrel. I was worried about tipping the whole thing over, but I got it done.

The rest of the day was filled with running errands inside and outside. I was learning what and where things were. No more critiques.

At the end of the day, I was given five quarters for my day's pay. I couldn't have been prouder or happier.

The second Saturday was pretty much just like the first, except that, at the end of the day, Max gave me four quarters. I stared at them in my hand and blurted out, "You gave me five quarters last week!"

Max stopped, looked at me for a few seconds. I stood my ground. He said, "I did?"

I said, "You did."

He gave me another quarter.

I went home and told my mother and everyone else that I had been given a raise after only one week.

MAGAZINES: Sid

There was only one time I remember my mother raising her voice to me. I was twelve.

"WHAT IS THIS?"

The "THIS" was a pile of magazines and the large cloth bag that they had come in.

"I'm going to go house to house and sell magazines", I proudly said.

Coming out of school that day, a gentleman standing next to a car hailed us. He went into a sales pitch about how we could make a lot of money by going from house to house selling magazines. The magazines he had were all familiar to me: Ladies Home Journal, Colliers, Saturday Evening Post.

A friend and I fell for the pitch. It involved no money from us. How could we miss? He filled up a bag for each of us with about two dozen magazines, had us sign a receipt, gave us his phone number, and we went home, dreaming of riches.

"NO, YOU'RE NOT!"

"What? Why not?"

"NEVER MIND WHY NOT. YOU BRING THOSE MAGAZINES BACK WHERE YOU GOT THEM AND FORGET ABOUT IT."

I stood wide-eyed with my mouth open, but something prevented me from saying anything. My mother was yelling at me! Shocked and disappointed, I put the magazines back in the bag, called the number I had, and returned the magazines.

I was too stunned to ask, so I never got an answer to my "Why not". Was she worried about the safety issues that might be involved? Did she think that having a son as a door-to-door salesman was an embarrassment? Did she think it would interfere with my working in the store?

My mother thought it was wrong, and that had to be enough for me.

WARTIME: David

Joey was drafted in September 1941, well before Pearl Harbor.

Eddie Walsh went into the Navy and other men were being drafted, too, so the Norwood Market was keeping me busy. It was convenient for Max that I was coming along. I had gone fairly quickly from trimming chuck bones to boning chucks.

This is an impeccably logical way to learn. The chuck bone is the backbone from the neck down through the first five ribs. This is part of the forequarter, meaning the cow or steer has been split in half down the spine and cut across at the last ribs. The rest of that half of the animal is called the hindquarter.

The foreleg and "breast" with the brisket, plate, hanger steak, skirt steak and flank steak have been removed and are not on the chuck. The chuck will lie flat on the cutting bench on the sawn vertebrae. Boning a chuck means taking all the meat off in one piece, which is then tied into a long cylinder with butcher's twine. You get three or four chuck pot roasts out of the cylinder and the trimmings go into hamburger.

You can't efficiently do a perfect job of taking the chuck off the bone. You could, but it would take two or three times as long, and after all, you need the trimmings for hamburger. There are dozens of little ins and outs where the white bone is covered with beef. Most of the trimming is done with the point of the boning knife and the beauty of the learning process is that, later, when you are boning a chuck you do a pretty good job on the ins and outs, because you know where they are from all that practice on trimming the bones. But you're not worried about being perfect, because again, you need trimmings for hamburg.

Through my junior and senior year in high school, I was boning and rolling a lot of chucks on Friday nights after the store closed at 6pm.

My hours on Friday were about 2pm to 9pm (school let out at 1:30). One of the big jobs on Friday after the doors were closed was taking all the fish and ice out of the window and the front case. The window display area was a sloping tile sink that drained at the front. It was packed with ice and fish was displayed most of the week. But Friday night it was all stripped, washed down with soap and water and deodorized because Saturday morning it would be packed with fresh ice and a meat and poultry display would be put out.

Here's the store's #1 household hint: the deodorizer was about half a bottle of vanilla diluted in about half a bucket of water.

At about 9 pm, my friends would show up at the store. Donny Bookman, my best friend, who had by then moved from Everett to Malden, came with Sidney Gelpey and Herby Siegel. We would go bowling candlepins nearby and eat hamburgs (now hamburgers) and sodas. I would pick up the tab on these Friday nights. It was easy for me. Probably the whole thing was five dollars.

The effect of paying me like an adult (looking back on this years later) made me more of an adult. That was good; that was Max giving me a sense of self-worth, without any parenting speeches. It had a less attractive side: it also kind of spoiled me about money, and oriented me to think it would always come easily if you were willing to work. Indeed, my generation was always able to get the next job, until the 1980's when mergers and downsizing were invented.

But I wouldn't trade what I got from Max for anything. Besides the Friday night routine, I inherited some of Joey's and some of Eddie's jobs, the veal cutlet and bracciolla cutting starting at 4:30 Saturday morning.

But when rationing came, the business changed. It wiped out the late Saturday nights. The morning was busy cutting up and packaging everything we had in the store and filling up brown paper bags with customers' names on them. Max had collected the ration books from most of our regular customers and worked hard to "take care of them."

We were cleaned out and cleaned up by 2pm.

Max edged into products he hadn't before, like sugar, which was rationed into the middle of 1947. We had had a small dairy case but we went into the butter business to take care of customers.

Luckily, we had been buying Rath Packing Company veal for years. Now, they had to cut us to one whole calf a week, hide and all. That was a weekly chore for me for a couple of years - skinning the calf. They came white, black, white and black, white and brown, and they were beautiful. Someone who tanned the hides took them each week. Fortunately, they were big. There are a lot of veal cutlets on two big hind legs. I don't think Max was involved in the black market, which unquestionably existed, but I think he did public relations with Canadian Club whiskey. He had several cases in a small room on the top floor of the Woodlawn Street house, and I saw him many mornings slip a couple of them under his overcoat on the way to Faneuil Hall.

Sid, who got the brunt of the pasting of stamps, says that Max bemoaned the fact that the books from last week never seemed to add up to what he needed to buy this week, so it was a struggle, but he was making money like everyone else. Fish was not rationed and that became busier than ever. Max was an innovator, too. He brought fresh tuna into the store

with its strange red-beef color. It scared some people, but some of those same people tried it.

PIN UPS: Sid

From 1939 to 1944 we lived at 93 Irving Street. We rented the top two floors of a three-story house. David and I shared a bedroom on the top floor. It was large enough for us to each have a desk. The only two windows were on the front of the house, leaving plenty of wall space.

I had no reason or desire to have pictures on the walls, so David had no competition about what he wanted.

What he wanted, and finally had, were at least a dozen pin-up posters on our walls.

Esquire Magazine and True Magazine were including the famous pin-ups of World War II by 1942. Esquire sent 9 million free magazines with pin-ups and no advertising to troops in 1942.

The most famous pin-up artists at the time were Alberto Vargas and George Petty. Their paintings were called Vargas (pronounced Varga) Girls and Petty Girls. A Petty Girl adorned the nose of the B-17 Bomber *Memphis Belle,* as well as thousands of locker doors during WWII.

David had only Vargas and Petty Girls.

Max rarely ever came up to our floor. He had no reason to.

So he surprised us both when, one day just before supper, he took a couple of steps into the room.

He stopped, looked around, and said, to no one in particular, "Ach, now I know why he's so crazy." And left.

HAMBURG: David

He knew it and everybody else knew it. Nobody could grind and display hamburg the way Max could. That is, nobody was as good as he was at catching the ground meat coming out of the big machine. There was a trick to catching it in your palm and moving your hand back and forth from the wrist so as to put a wave in the meat. Then you gently put it into the tray.

Nobody was as good as Max at putting out a beautiful display in the deep white porcelain trays with the blue edging. It looked very inviting.

It didn't look that difficult to do, but we all found out that it wasn't easy.

Also. If you were one of the sons, you had to wait a long time before you were allowed to grind hamburg.

Dalrymple and other grownup help were allowed to do it because obviously Max couldn't be in the store every minute.

Sid recalls when he was about fifteen and already cutting meat, that he was asking over and over, pestering Max, to grind hamburg. Max always said no.

Then one day, paying his customary homage to the Muse of Drama, he said okay.

Sid, a little stunned, but eager, listened carefully and watched as Max showed him the motion and said several times, "The main thing is when you put it in the platter, don't pat it down."

This didn't have to be explained. You knew the hamburg looked better with the spontaneous, almost fluffy appearance that the Max method gave it. We had all seen pressed-down heavy-looking hamburg, and it lost out to Max's in attractiveness. And we sold a lot of it.

Anyway, Max said again, "Whatever you do, don't pat it down." Then, heading for the swinging doors to go out front, once again, "Don't forget. Don't pat it down."

Sid speaks somewhat in awe of what happened next.

He was just finishing filling the big tray as Max came back through the swinging doors, and Sid was PATTING IT DOWN!

"I was thunderstruck. I don't know why I did it. There's Max, like every boss in the history of the world, who's always standing there when you do something wrong. It wasn't about him. It was about me. I had this terrible pain in my chest that I had let him down. It affected the way I worked the rest of my life."

Funny things were happening in the store all the time. David and I were really puzzled when Max took a shine to a tall, gawky boy he had hired named Harold Clapper. Harold was a little older than I was.

It might be that he ran to do whatever Max wanted. Max got a kick out of him. One day Arthur said, "Harold, take that wooden bucket and fill it with water and bring it to the stove so we can cook some lobsters in it."

Harold took the wooden bucket and filled it with water and brought it to the stove in the back room.

A couple of us were cutting meat in the back room.

Harold says, "Would you guys give me a hand getting this bucket up onto the stove?"

We looked at him, the bucket, the gas stove, and each other. We said nothing and kept working with our backs to him.

He said, "Come on, guys, this bucket is heavy."

We said nothing.

"Please?"

We still said nothing.

He finally got it. He knew we weren't going to help him, or anybody, put a wooden bucket on to a stove that had a gas flame.

Max was mostly serious. But he was always ready for some fun.

After he had wrung out some woman who had asked if the fish was fresh, he would say, "Oh, I had fun with her. Did you hear that? Oh, that was fun."

He always had time for these shenanigans, and children did not escape his mischief. There was a space between the front window display and the front display case.

Sometimes a six or seven year old boy would slip into the space in order to watch the fish cutting. Max would turn his head to the boy and say, "Would you eat a dead fish?"

The boy, surprised and suddenly guilty, would blurt out, "NO!" Max would say, "What do you think your mother just bought?" The boy is now completely rattled.

Max was not above repeating jokes he had heard. He had two lines ready if we passed by a cemetery. "There's people dying to get in there", or, "there are people dying now that never died before."

Driving past a rich-looking house and you said, "Those people have a lot of money", he would say,"It doesn't show how much money they've got, only how much money they had."

One episode needs telling: I came to dinner one night with dirty face and hands. Ma said, "Go wash up." I said, "Why should I wash up? I'm only going to get dirty again." Pa put his nose near mine and said, calmly, "Then why do you want to eat? You're only going to get hungry again. WASH UP!"

Then there was the time a customer asked about how David was doing in New York. Max says, "Oh, he's doing just fine. He's making a living from writing. He writes home for money."

BAR MITZVAHS: Sid

In July 1943 I was the last of the Bennett boys to be Bar Mitzvahed.

I had been to Hebrew School in the late Thirties in Revere, Massachusetts because Max was in one of his Synagogue disputes in Everett. I took an afternoon bus five times a week for about two years until I was liberated. The bus rides were an adventure, but the school was not.

I learned the printed and handwritten alphabet, including the symbols underneath the letters, which helped the pronunciation. I could read very well. I never learned what a single word meant. Translations were not part of the curriculum. At the time, I did not care.

As long as Max was part of the Malden Street Synagogue, I would go there for Holiday Services. His participation there was an on-again off-again situation and so was mine. Until I figured out how to avoid it, I had to sit and try to follow the service and I had to sit for the speeches. Max, as President, in his large linen Tallis with black bands, spoke in Yiddish, as did some of the other elders. The speeches were mostly about raising money for the Synagogue or the Free Loan Society or some charity. If we had a Rabbi, I don't remember that. If there were speeches about interpreting the Bible, I would not have known about it.

Early in 1943 Pa brought me to the Irving Street Shul to be tutored afternoons by Mr. Promisel. I learned the benedictions, the Saturday passage of the Torah (Bible) for my birthday, and how to put on Tefillin. I just did as I was told. Nothing was ever explained. No one ever translated my Torah passage. I simply knew it was traditional, and happily went along.

I asked if Joe and David had done the same thing. I was told that they certainly were Bar Mitzvahed. They did go to Hebrew School in Everett and Joe had his service at the same Irving Street Shul. But Max took David to a Malden, Massachusetts Synagogue which held very early Saturday morning services. Max had to work Saturdays, so this was the only way it could be done.

I had heard about how some boys had large parties at which they had to give a speech, which usually ended with, "Today I am a man." There were lots of gifts for the birthday boy. There were jokes about how many fountain pens were given as gifts. One had the birthday boy say, "Today I am a fountain pen."

Joe and David did not have parties. None of my friends had parties, and I was never invited to a relative's party. So there were no expectations.

There were only a few regulars at my service. No family members were there. They were all working in the store. The only person who was there who mattered to me was a beautiful and brilliant girl in my classes that I had a huge unrequited crush on. I was surprised to see her and, dunce that I was, I never did anything about it.

I got through it. I walked to the store where everyone made a fuss about the Bar Mitzvah boy. I celebrated by going to a double feature. I hadn't expected a party, so I didn't miss it.

Years later, when I married a non-Jewish girl, there were relatives who said I did that because no one came to my Bar Mitzvah. What nonsense. I was never instructed enough to become interested or observant. As David reports, I used to say, "Nobody tells me anything."

COMMUNITY SERVICE: Sid

One of the principles of Judaism is service to the community. Max did more than his share. He left a five page chronological summary of "the years and time" he spent in Everett.

Soon after moving to Everett in 1917, he sought out the Jewish life there. He became and remained a member of his first synagogue, the Congregation B'nai Israel on Irving Street, Everett, throughout his life, even though he joined other congregations.

A couple of years after Joe started to go to the Everett Hebrew School they expanded to become the Everett Hebrew School and Community Center. Max was asked to serve on the Board of Directors as Treasurer. Six years later he was elected President and served until 1934. He then writes, "I took a rest."

His "rest' included serving as Recording Secretary for the Everett Hebrew Free Loan Association and as President of the Araner Aid Association. The Free Loan Associations would make loans free of interest to local residents who would usually add a "contribution" when paying back the loan. Aran was the original name of the village where Max was born.

Not only did Max serve the Jewish Community, his business experience helped him to serve two years as the President of the Everett Retail Grocers Association.

By 1940 he joined the Congregation Tifereth Israel Synagogue, always called the Malden Street Shul, and rose in the ranks there, also. He was on the Board of Directors, then Chairman. He was Chairman when he asked Lillian to form a Sisterhood. This was another one of Max's controversial moves, but she proved to be good at it. She had made friends with enough women to organize them and start the Sisterhood.

As Vice President he made more controversy by trying to raise money to replace the 1912 building, against the President's advice. They raised enough money to start the project, but new pledges dried up. For a number of years there were some rusting steel beams over a large hole in front of the building. It was called "Bennett's Folly". Eventually, in 1967, the new synagogue was built.

However, in 1982, the building was totally destroyed by fire. The incident became national news when three Roman Catholic fire chaplains risked their lives to rescue the Torah scrolls. The new building was re-dedicated in 1983.

In 1950 Max sold the Norwood Market, resigned from the Malden Street Shul, and went on his first trip to Israel. He had gone back to the small Irving Street Shul, where he soon became President of the B'nai Israel Free Loan Association, and later, President of the Congregation.

After he sold the Circle Market in Arlington, he put some energy into the Everett Zionist Association and attended conventions in New York and Israel. The Association rewarded him with a breakfast in his honor and presented him with a travel bag for his journeys.

Despite his problems with the Malden Street Shul, they gave him a gold watch for his service.

We never had direct knowledge of his quarrels with the other members, but we can guess. Some of his problems must have come from his ideas on how things should be done, the same problem he had with his children. His views on religious subjects were always on the liberal side of a discussion. For instance, we do know that, contrary to the Orthodox attitude that

Jesus never existed, Max treated him as a real person who was as good as any of the prophets.

Max spent his last years with his companions at services, meetings, and discussions at the Congregation B'nai Israel, otherwise known as the Irving Street Shul.

Ford Hall Forum: Sid

Max once took Joe to a Red Sox baseball game. I guess he felt he had then made his American cultural contribution for his sons, because he never took David or me to any sports event.

His cultural contributions to me, however, were in the form of marvelous evenings when he took me to the Ford Hall Forum in Boston in the mid 1940's. He must have taken Joe and David, but I have no memory of that. Max put me, a teenager, in the midst of his peers and made me feel very important.

The Ford Hall Forum in Boston is "the oldest free public lecture series in the United States." Their mission is "to promote freedom of speech and foster an informed and engaged citizenry through free public presentations of lectures, debates, and discussions (quotes from Wikipedia)."

The evening I remember fairly clearly was a lecture by someone on the subject of who killed Jesus. He took the point of view of a detective going through the evidence to prove that it was not the Jews who killed Jesus, - it was the Romans who killed Jesus. Max said that he neatly sidestepped the issue of whether any Jews contributed to the event.

The other evenings are vague memories of discussions with an inevitable liberal point of view. Even speakers with an opposite view were politely listened to and questioned.

Max was more than liberal. He was a socialist. He even bragged about how wonderful Russia was. But, in the late thirties, when Joe and some of his friends contemplated joining the Communist Party, it was Max who talked him out of it.

These discussions mirrored our family efforts at talking about the latest political and social events. There should be no doubt that this is where my own views on life and living come from. As a member of an oppressed minority, it is easy to align yourself with other groups in the same situation. Being made aware of The Golden Rule provides an all-encompassing way to behave.

Max brought something with him from his early years to be interested in politics and make him an avid New York Times reader. He was the influence that made us all interested in what he was interested in.

THREE SONS IN UNIFORM: David

I would have started cutting meat in the store by the time I was 15, in any event, but World War II speeded things up. Max's meat-cutters were enlisting and getting drafted. Eddie Walsh went into the Navy, and part-timers were scarce.

My uncles, my mother's brothers, enlisted before they were to be drafted. Henry was a cook in the 8th Air Force in England and Belgium, and Frankie was shipped to North Africa. Frankie's company was traveling to the front on a train which was strafed by German fighter planes.

Frankie, along with many others, was returned almost immediately to the United States because of "shell-shock," a term left over from World War I.

They were all heroes to me. Another hero was Auntie Bea, who was to marry Henry later. She joined the WAVES (The WAVES were Women Accepted for Volunteer Emergency Services, the U.S. Navy's answer to the WACS - the Women's Army Corps). Joey was among the first peacetime draftees, and went into the service in September 1941, months before Pearl Harbor. He was 23, I was 15, and Sidney was 11.

Joey was put into the Infantry, the Ohio State Buckeye Division.

In civilian life, Joey had a problem with flat feet, and there were some hopeful thoughts by my Mother that the bad feet would keep Joey out of the service. But, ironically, marching in the infantry boots in Basic Training in Tennessee cured the problem.

It was a miracle.

Max also had trouble with his feet at one time, so Sid and I wondered if we were next, but we weren't.

Another story from Joey's Basic Training was that the Northern boys rebelled against the spicy Southern food served in the essentially southern culture of the Regular Army in Tennessee. And they got the food changed!

This impressed the hell out of me, age 15, and even more so once I got into the service myself.

Joey's group in basic was full of college graduates, and they were the generation that witnessed the Depression, flirted with Communism, and volunteered to fight in Spain for the Republic against the Fascist. Maybe they just weren't taking any crap from anyone.

Another story from that time was that Joey was picked to talk to the troops on "Why We Fight." Somebody had actually looked at the records and saw he was a history major from Harvard.

I wasn't there, but I know exactly what he covered, even if they gave him a prepared lecture. The reason I knew was because I had once asked him, 'What's different about America?" And he said, "The separation of powers. The checks and balances in the Constitution. The balance of powers among the Executive, the Legislative, and the Judiciary is unique. Each one keeps an eye on the other two, and you have a chance for everyone to stay honest. That was the genius of the Founding Fathers." That was worth fighting to keep, wasn't it? This stayed with me my whole life, augmented by a course in school they don't give anymore, called Civics.

I kept wondering why they didn't make Joey an officer. He was a damn genius, wasn't he?

I didn't know much about how the world works. They didn't need geniuses. They needed mortar spotters in the South Pacific, and that's where they sent Joey.

My parents were probably a fairly ordinary couple in their reaction to having a son in the Pacific, but it showed more on my mother than on Max. I don't know the biology of these things, but that's definitely when her shiny black hair began to turn gray.

Mostly, they were just like everyone else once the war actually started, totally immersed in the "war effort." It was a thrilling time of unity. There was nothing to question. Japan bombed us, didn't they?

And we were already deep into helping England. Then Germany and Italy declared war on the United States. We were practically in their war, the way we had been sending war material to England even before Pearl Harbor.

So WWII was not like Korea and Viet Nam, when there was plenty to question.

There were a lot of loyal patriotic American boys who saw it as their duty to go into the service during Korea and Viet Nam, but everyone in the country at that time was cheated of the WWII feeling; hour-by-hour and day-by-day, that we were all pulling together, the feeling that came automatically in World War II. For the most part, everyone went about their business in a quiet way, with a confidence, giving up their sons and daughters to the Service, and putting up with rationing. A symbol of the times to me was how seriously we joined in on projects like gathering "tin foil."

I remember, along with Sid, separating the foil from the paper from cigarette packages and gum wrappers, and rolling it into baseball-sized lumps that Lillian turned in somewhere. The foil was not just from Max's cigarettes, but from packages we found on the street and in trash. I never saw that calm, united look on every face again until September

11th 2001, when I was writing this book, and the World Trade Center buildings in New York City and the Pentagon in Washington, D.C. were hit by hijacked airplanes.

It was the biggest shock for the nation Since Pearl Harbor, and indeed it was a Pearl Harbor. I watched these horrific events all morning on television, and saw in the days that followed that everyone had that look that I remembered from WWII, and in the next few days, I heard both men and women say often, "I wish I could do something."

New Yorkers lined up by the thousands to give blood, as a way of "doing something."

Even as a teenager, I was sentimentally and intellectually patriotic, and stayed that way the rest of my life. I was very clear about being excited at being in this unique country. Surely a contributing factor, not realized until decades later, was Max's "Only in America" which he said both with great gravity (two Jewish boys from Everett getting into Harvard in 1934), and sometimes derisively (the funny Ponzi pyramid scheme), which a lot of people fell for.

It was in this mode that I enlisted eagerly in the Army Air Corps at the beginning of my senior year in High School, with the prospect of being taken at the end of the year, when I would be 18. We were called High School Air Cadets and received small wings crossed vertically by a propeller, which I proudly pinned on a lapel whenever I wore a Sports jacket.

There was an implication, or perhaps it was only an inference, that we would be flight officers. Your parents didn't have to sign on this deal, and I enlisted without discussing it with them, but they never complained.

This was a typical non-discussion event in the family. It never occurred to me that they would disapprove, and they didn't. They were outwardly stoical, but I'm sure my mother prayed that the war would be over before I went in.

As for me, I had a crystal-clear vision of flying a fighter or a bomber in the South Pacific just ahead of Joey's frontline, and wiping out the enemy threatening him. The clearest fantasy I ever had.

There was a special new course in High School, called Aeronautics. Mr. Mahan had gone to MIT on a leave to learn meteorology and navigation so he could teach them to us. So my fantasy reformed into being a navigator on a bomber, and I had another happy year in school and cutting meat for Max.

Graduation Day was June 6th, 1944. D-Day. On July 5th I entered the Air Corps. I don't think any of the High School Air Cadets became officers. Certainly I didn't. I trained a lot as an enlisted armorer-gunner on B-17s and B29s, but never saw combat. Enlisting was the greatest thing I did in my lifetime, except for proposing to my wife Jane.

Sid got a Master's degree in Communications from Boston University in May 1955 and with a pregnant wife, he volunteered for the draft in June 1955. It wasn't until I was writing this book that I asked him, 'Wouldn't Stephen have been your exemption?" He said, "I think that might have worked, but I wanted to go, get it over with and start my career. Joey had gone, you had gone, I thought it was 'payback'. I've always believed in national conscription. I believe everyone owes the country something. I'm glad I did it."

I agree.

I think there's something about being the son of immigrants that maybe makes you feel more keenly that you "owe the country something."

THE CURSE: Sid

It was a bright and beautiful day. Summer, 1947. I still had one more year of high school. David was home from the University of Missouri, where he was studying to be a writer.

One of our summer activities was to go to the dogs - that is, to the Wonderland Dog track in Revere. My friends and I would go, David and his friends would go, and occasionally, we would all go together. We would most likely end the evening with a trip to any one of a number of great ice cream places in Revere, or Lynn, or Swampscott. In order to get a conversation going with a girl behind the counter, I would ask for a ginger ale frappe. First, they would say that they couldn't do that - it would explode in the mixer. After I said it wouldn't, they would get a manager, and if I said I would clean it up, they would finally do it. It was delicious, but I never did get any dates from it.

Wonderland published a daily program of the evening's races with more information than you would ever want about the dogs. The program was easy to get in Everett Square.

It was a slow day in the store. Max was off somewhere with one of his business friends. So I got the dog book and brought it back to the store.

David and I were at the end of the display cases, going through the book, picking dogs to bet on that night.

Artie was at his usual place, cutting fish at the front of the store surrounded by that wonderful tile and the ice-filled fish case. He had the eternal cigarette in his mouth. The trained ash would get longer and longer. The smoke was going up into his eyes, making him squint and bend his head out of the way of the smoke. He would cough a little, too.

He knew what we were doing.

Without looking up or changing the pace with his knife, he made his calm, slow, pronouncement, emphasizing each word.

"YOU GUYS ARE NEVER GONNA HAVE ANY MONEY EXCEPT WHAT YOU EARN BY THE SWEAT OF YOUR BROW."

If you put me in a witness stand, I would swear that the sky suddenly grew dark and there was a clap of thunder. We were cursed.

The curse was never broken, not even years later when I won a salami at a picnic.

THREE SONS AND A DAUGHTER: David

In the days of the Norwood Market, there was a kind of odd dance going on built around arguments in the store between Max and each of his sons. These arguments never occurred at home.

Each son brought a different style to the situation. Joey, a first-born - who are traditionally the most respectful of parents' authority and don't show the rebelliousness of the later arrivals - would walk out on a budding argument.

I was glad to be a third-born, since they seem to be more free and easy. I thought Sid also had some of the characteristics of the third child. My own theory is that the first-born is a little more uptight and edgy because he is the one the parents lean on, the one they use up their nervousness on. By the time Sid and I came along, Max and Lillian had used up all their extra anxiety on Joey and Sylvia. Thinking back, I can't believe the freedom I had. At about 12 I loved swimming and found there was a pool at the Boys Club in Charlestown. It was the next town over, yet I was allowed to go there by bus and subway at night.

In any case, in the store, Joey was the most respectful when exasperated by Max. He didn't argue. As soon as Max hit some hot button of Joey's, his face would flush and he would hit a strong stride right out from behind the counter and out the front door, bloody white apron and bloody white coat, and disappear.

He would buy a milk shake or a frappe from Giaccobbe's Drug Store on the corner, and walk over into Roody's Millinery, almost directly across the street from the Norwood Market, and owned by Rose Rood, mother of Bernice Rood, Sylvia's friend and classmate, and Lenny Rood, my friend and classmate. Joey would go into the backroom through the fabric divider, and cool off, talking with Bernice. Years later, Joey and Bernice were married. Many years later, when I asked Bernice if Joey talked about Max and the store when he was in the millinery, she said no.

I never walked out. My style was to stand toe-to-toe with Max and, without really showing any disrespect, answer him evenly but sometimes with voice raised. Max loved to look out at any customers who were witnessing this foolishness, and say, "It's all right, I'm only his father." Like a lot of things in the store, it all had elements of theatricality, or show biz.

Sid was the genius of the three of us. He already had the reputation as the family comedian, and he would turn a store argument into a joke. He would do a childish, ridiculous Lou Costello, clowning and apologizing, "I don't know why I did that." Everyone would crack up, including Max.

When I was writing this book, I called Sid and asked him what the hell we used to argue about with Max. I couldn't remember to save my life. Sid couldn't remember, either, but after we talked a while, we agreed it was stuff like Max questioning why one of us was bringing out a fresh platter of hamburg or pork Chops from the cooler. He wouldn't have brought one out at that moment. It was all about why and how things were done.

It was a kind of jousting, or a wolf and cubs mock fighting, wrestling to learn how to do it seriously later.

Rarely, one of us was undisputedly correct about some fact. Then Max would scowl and say, "The chickens don't like to be taught by the eggs."

All three of us had different ways of dealing with Max. All three had confidence and security to spare. Nobody's sense of worth was damaged. I think you had to give Max credit. He let us exercise our identity muscles, and we got more identity as time went by.

The arguments were absolutely over when they were over. There was no rancor or even memory of it a minute later, although maybe a little with Joey. I think he carried a heavier burden than Sid and me. Probably things between Max and Joey changed forever when he spoke up at 16 and said he couldn't carry the weight of Harvard and Yeshiva at the same time.

At that time, I think Max began to realize all his sons would be going to college and that none of us would enter the business.

So I think there was a strong undercurrent of Max experiencing territorialism.

It was "our store" for purposes of taking pride in it, and I believe we got a lot of our identity from it, but there was never any question about whose store it was. None of this was articulated at the time, I realized later when we became adults. Meanwhile we were getting extremely valuable training, which was also not understood at the time.

When I got into heavy discussions and arguments in business meetings later in life, I always had a cool head because of the training with Max. And I was always more comfortable with clients the higher up they were, and most comfortable with the top guy, the "Max" of that particular Company.

I know Max enjoyed us talking back. He got a kick out of it. I caught him bragging about it once to a friend on the phone. "Oh, you should hear them talk back," and laugh.

The territorialism idea was borne out convincingly several times.

We had a big fish business, and Joey campaigned for a while for Max to put in fish-frying equipment, but he wouldn't. His stated reason was that he would be competing with Eddie Gold's Delicatessen up Norwood Street, and Eddie was a friend. Eddie had the only fish & chips business in Everett, as far as I knew. I thought of Joey's idea after World War II, when fish fry and sub shops proliferated in Everett. It seemed like every other block had a fish-fry place or a sub shop.

There was another thing Joey wanted and didn't get. In September 1941, Joey was drafted. So he wanted his last Saturday in the store to be his. He wanted to run the store for one day without Max being there.

Max's patriotism wasn't strong enough to overcome his territorialism. The answer was no.

When Max decided suddenly in 1950, after 20 years on Norwood Street, that he wanted to sell the store and go visit his brother in Israel, he consulted nobody.

Sid always recalled with some pain, that he and Arthur Dalrymple could have run the store in the summer, the slowest business time of the year, while Max was in Israel. Why give up a successful store that way?

But there was never any discussion. In fact, it turned out Max had bought a store in Arlington on Massachusetts Avenue before he even left, and it was waiting for him when he got back from Israel after a few months.

That puzzled Sid even more. Why a small supermarket? We all knew Max was brilliant at choosing sides of beef for their quality. Sid's idea was that Max should open a small specialty meat shop in a wealthy town like Newton and cater to housewives who wanted to guarantee their meat dinners would please their husbands and their guests.

That discussion never went very far, either.

Things conspired, and my mother conspired, to put me into that Arlington store. I had just graduated from the University of Missouri, and discovered I needed a pilonidal cyst operation. I came home and Sylvia got me a VA doctor friend to do the operation. This operation site is at the base of the spine, so that means for a few weeks you are lying on your stomach listening to music and reading while you heal.

I remember lying on the floor in the living room and, it seems as if it were daily, my mother dropping by to stand over me and do a sort of Chinese water drip torture. She was telling me constantly how Max could really use me in the new Arlington store. This of course meant that Max had said that to her.

But finally I went in. The school year had started and I couldn't start on my Master's Degree at Missouri, so what the hell, I went in.

Without any discussion, I took over as a grocery manager, as there was no one doing that. I figured out pretty fast that we could only have one facing, or row, of something like Campbell's Tomato Soup. A real supermarket might have 6 or 8 facings of the one soup. But if we were going to offer everything in the store, one facing was the limit on everything.

This made for a lot of work. I remember working until 9:30 and 10 at night stocking shelves. I had some kind of an urge to get the word out that there was a store called Circle Market. I suddenly became a direct mail person. I had no idea that's what you would call it, and I had no idea that a few years later I would start a career in advertising in New York City.

I wrote 50-100 word flyers and went to a printer who set type for a sheet about 5 inches by 8 inches. They were marvels of a variety of sizes and fonts of type. They looked like little circus posters. In later years I would torture myself with regret for not having saved one of them. I got a complete list of the citizenry of Arlington from City Hall, complete with addresses, and stuffed a few hundred envelopes with the flyers every two weeks or so.

The brilliant advertising theme was that "There must be a reason" why people were coming to the Circle Market. The reason was the great meat and produce offered by Max Bennett. As for the groceries, a can of Campbell's Soup was a can of Campbell's Soup no matter where you bought it.

I scouted the four big nearby supermarkets and matched their prices on the groceries. The flyers were working. People came in to try the store, and mentioned getting the flyers. On the flyers, I also offered delivery and a number for ordering over the phone

I had discovered that this was not one of Max's brilliant buys. The place had things wrong with it. It was a small supermarket; you couldn't use regular shopping carts; they were too big for two of them to pass in the aisles. So we had small-sized shopping carts. But even small ones were trouble.

Apparently, although Max had a great feel for a lot of things, he didn't have a great feel for supermarkets. Why would he? I don't think he ever shopped in one. I had a good idea. If the aisles were jammed even with just a few Customers and a few carts in use, how about keeping people out of the store? I hired two teen-angers with cars to come in after high school and advertised phone orders and deliveries.

It was unquestionably a success. We were paying the boys, and the customers were cheerfully paying a dollar per order and also tip. Suddenly, one day after a couple months of this, Max stopped the deliveries. I arrived at work and saw a sign in the window, "No Delivery" I never asked him why he did that. I was too prideful and ultimately didn't care. And after all, it was his store, right?

I was gone within a month, off to New York and a new life.

*****

SID:

At the same time that Max was opening the Circle Market, I was starting college at Boston University, determined on a career in theatre. I worked weekends unless schoolwork or rehearsals interfered.

I had graduated high school in 1948, but because of my procrastination, I worked a year and applied to schools before I was admitted to the University of Colorado to become an engineer. By Christmas vacation I had become inextricably involved in theatre and came home to apply to Boston University.

Within that first year, Max and I had an argument about something that went over the top. I felt awful about it, and tried to think of a way to stop the nonsense.

I finally realized that it took two to argue, so I was determined not to argue anymore. I would just shut my mouth.

This was not as easy as I thought. It took a period of over two months before I could totally keep my mouth shut. After another few months, I realized there was a change in my attitude.

What had happened was that I had begun not to care about what was going on. I knew now that one of the reasons there were arguments was because Joey,

David, and I cared about the store and Max, and wanted things to be better. So I made things better by caring enough to keep my mouth shut.

*****

DAVID:

In 1951, the importance of the Circle Market diminished when Sylvia, in the midst of a blooming nursing career, was diagnosed with intestinal cancer, later known as colon cancer.

After two operations done at the Framingham Hospital, near where she worked and keeping it from Max and Lillian, and staying with her nurse friend Anne, she finally couldn't work anymore and came home to Everett and told Max and Lillian.

We began a long year with the whole family pretty whacked up. Sylvia was at home with Lillian. There was a constant problem of finding drugs to help her with her pain. Sidney became a sort of drug dealer. Even though he had prescriptions, he had to find drug stores that had the drugs and believed his prescription was legitimate.

I was coming home from New York on Trailways buses almost every weekend. Max went to work at the Circle Market, appearing stoical but unquestionably broken up inside.

I remember Anne trying to tell us something about handling the situation, and thinking that we were not up to it, and I think she was right.

But we were doing the best we knew how. Lillian was always strong in adverse situations and she was that way throughout Sylvia's last year.

Sidney, only 21, performed handsomely chasing the drugs that were so important.

*****

SID:

After Sylvia's second operation, Anne and David took me aside one night at her house to tell me that Sylvia had cancer that was no longer operable. She had a year or two to live. I was not to tell anyone, especially Ma and Pa. It was one of those minutes you don't forget.

I got into bed that night and I knew my monologues with God were over. I cried myself to sleep that night and it was years before I ever cried again.

It became my job to get the drugs Sylvia needed. A prescription would appear for Demerol, or Morphine, or Dilaudid, so I went to fill it. I used the drug stores in Everett for a while. I always got questioning looks and a few questions. I usually told them to call the Doctor if they had a problem.

Later, when I had to go out of town, Herbie Siegel, one of David's close friends who was now a pharmacist, would help. If he didn't have a supply, he would call a pharmacist friend to fill a prescription.

One day, before Sylvia came to stay in Everett and before Lillian and Max knew the truth about what was happening, she needed to go back to Framingham. Max wanted to drive her, but she insisted that I take her. Max was just as insistent as she was. I watched this battle with my heart in my throat, ready to cry. Finally, Sylvia convinced him that it was better if I took her.

I know he must have had unasked questions, but simply gave in.

She knew she would need an injection on the way and did not want him to see it. She sat in the back seat that day and we hardly spoke.

Sylvia died October 6, 1952, two weeks before she would have been 32 years old. I had just gotten home from trying to visit her in the hospital when I took the call.

Her doctor told me and said that it was for the best - her pain was over. I had to agree, but I was still angry.

I told Ma, and she collapsed into a chair, crying. I went to the Irving Street Shul to tell Pa. He made it home before he lost control. He was able to call a good friend who came to help him make calls and the arrangements for the funeral.

*****

DAVID:

She was a beautiful heavy woman, reminiscent of Camryn Mannheim when serious and Rosie O' Donnell when she was clowning around. She was a great loving fun sister to me and I didn't know the depth of my feelings for some time. I had no idea of the depth of Max's feelings until many years later.

As for Lillian, the most angry I ever saw her was after Sylvia died and we were sitting Shiva in the house and this poor young rabbi came by to get himself scalded by Lillian's stern demand that he explain this tremendous loss. He was wise enough not to try.

Surely Sylvia's death was a factor in the Circle Market's demise.

The store was not successful, and Max sold it at a low price a couple years later and went into a real retirement. He worked for other storeowners, acquaintances from 40 years of the business. He went his own way, visiting Israel some more, and living in the old two-family on Woodlawn Street, busily rounding up elderly Jewish men to make up a minyan at the Irving Street Synagogue. What the toll was on Lillian, I don't know. But I think it was wearing to live all those years with someone who was always his own man, and rarely discussed personal feelings with family members. He had animated discussions with other storeowners, but that was largely them asking him for advice, because he was respected as a creative and successful retailer.

Frema, who married Lenny Rood, was a real friend of Sylvia's, and who adored Max, moved to the West Coast and became a psychological therapist. She said of Max, "Sylvia was the love of his life." Without a doubt, she was right. She laughed when she saw the title of my book about Max and we had a serious discussion about the Oedipal Complex.

It wasn't brain surgery to see a benign rivalry between the father and sons. But beyond that, Frema thought, there was an ordinary masculine competitiveness, and a disappointment that the sons would not carry on and perpetuate what the father had started. Of course he wanted all of us to go to college, and realized at some point the irony that we would go on to new lives after that and not join him in the business. He wanted that, but if you weren't going to join him in the business, why should you have a say in it?

Frema said there was also a factor of the father being unable to insure the safety of his sons and his daughter. "If you go forth into any world I have not explored, I cannot protect you, I cannot ensure your safety."

There were many factors, unarticulated by the parties at the time, and not analyzed for decades, and never by Max. He was a self-made man, who had listened to his own counsel only, and had taken chances and been successful (until Arlington). Why would he give up power to his sons, especially when

they were a little frightening, when they were so smart?

MORE: Sid

Soon after Sylvia died, Max and Lillian got more bad news. Joe was diagnosed with Multiple Sclerosis. None of us knew anything about MS, but we soon found out more than we wanted to know.

He and Bernice were both teaching at Quincy High School. He was a vocational guidance counselor and she was teaching English and running the drama club. Their oldest son Alan was four and Paul was one.

The Veteran's Administration decided that he had contacted the disease sometime during his three years in the South Pacific: at Guadalcanal, Bougainville, or Luzon, where he was wounded.

He became part of a small group of veterans with MS who had the benefit of every kind of medicine and program available.

The disease took over very slowly. As the years went on, he needed a cane, and then a wheelchair. None of it stopped Bernice and some very good friends from taking him on trips to California and even Israel. She took excellent care of him, and I'm sure her care made his life longer. All the men who were diagnosed with him were gone long before he was.

*****

There was more bad news for Max and Lillian in 1953. I had fallen in love with a girl who was not Jewish. I met her at Boston University when she was a cast member of one of our shows.

About a week after I told them we were getting married, Max sat me down in the kitchen and very calmly explained to me what it would mean if I married this girl, and all the reasons why no Jewish boy should marry someone who was not Jewish. I was affected by this long talk and I understood everything he said about Judaism. But Sylvia's death had completed my feelings about religion. I had made up my mind and would not, could not, change it.

I know I hurt him and my mother deeply.

*****

The next bad news waited until 1963.

Life had gone on. I was married, had children that in time Max and Lillian loved. Grandchildren often overcome tradition, especially when the grandparents are practical and forgiving. It also helps if the grandchildren are happy and loveable. David married a girl who was not Jewish and also had children that Max and Lillian loved for the same reasons.

Max finally gave up the Circle Market in 1957 when he got Social Security. He worked part time for many of the friends he had in the business, so he kept busy. He also made more trips to Israel.

David's advertising career kept him in New York. My theatre career carried me to Canada, Long Island, and New York. The fact that we were making a living at what we loved was good enough for Max. I know he was as proud of us then as he was when we were meat cutters, although he never said it to us. We know he was proud of us because the people he told would tell us.

The problem now was that Lillian was failing. The high blood pressure and heart problems finally caught up to her and she died in 1963 of heart failure.

We had come to visit her at the hospital. She was in an oxygen tent. Through the door, she was happy to see our kids.

Once more, I was home when the call came. Once again, I got Max at the Irving Street Shul. He was calmer this time, but still very upset. He had me call his friend who came right away.

There were many more people at the funeral service than I expected. There were people standing outside the funeral home. It was easy to forget about the many years that Max and Lillian had spent not only in business in Everett, but in all the community and religious organizations they supported and worked for. The attendance was a tribute to them both.

*****

By 1971 Joey had been through a few emergency sessions with pneumonia. Bernice made sure that the doctors did their best to get him home each time. Finally, just a few days short of his fifty-fourth birthday, he died.

My family and I were living on Cape Cod, so I did not see Max until the next day at the funeral. He seemed stoic, detached, and resigned to the fact that these tragedies were going to continue to happen. Even though he had once said that he believed that God was Nature, he believed that the Bible and the Talmud set out the rules for living and he was trying to follow them.

FINDING MAX: Sid

In 2001, when the Ellis Island records were made available, I tried to find Max's arrival. His case was special, because we knew he did not enter the United States at that time. He was sent back, evidently because the family agent had not paid for a full fare. I found no trace of him, and a letter to the administration was never answered.

I thought that if we could trace his entry, then perhaps we could get more information on what happened to the family in Aran during World War II. We had a good idea of what happened, but no confirmation.

We knew he disembarked in Boston from the Ivernia on September 6, 1906. However, the Port of Boston does not have online records similar to Ellis Island. So the matter was laid to rest.

In 2006 I was made aware of the fact that the Family History Centers had records of ship's manifests that were available to the public.

Max had told us that the family name in Lithuania was Benetovich. In going through the Little Blue Suitcase, I found other spellings: Benatevetz, Banetevetz, Bentovicz, etc.

There was another spelling, not in those papers, that turned out to be very interesting for both his citizenship application and to help my search. The story that follows is almost implausible.

The source of this information was Arthur Golnick, who contacted us in 1997. As a boy, he remembered Max coming to New York to visit his family. He was trying to connect our families by proving that Max's mother Shaina was Arthur's grandmother. He was retired from working for the United States Government and was able to get records we never thought about. However, he never was able to prove the connection.

Arthur sent us copies of some information he uncovered. In those papers, I found two letters that were written by relatives for Max to apply for citizenship. There were also government letters saying, in effect, that there was no evidence of him having come to the U.S.

There was, incredibly, a piece of paper certified by some clerk, that said that indeed, a 'Benjalovitz, Mordche' had arrived on the Ivernia. Benjalovitz? Where does that come from?

Since we have his citizenship papers, this evidence must have been enough to prove that he had entered the United States when he said he did.

In 2006, searching for a Family History Center, I found one only six miles away in Brewster. I went there, was led to a computer, given some instruction, and found the Ivernia arrival late August 1906. Expecting to go through hundreds of pages of the manifest, I started to look slowly and carefully for any spelling, especially this Benjalovitz.

I almost missed it on page 148. Almost illegible, it does look like Benjalovitz, Mordche. Is it our Max? His line of information shows that it is: Age: 16, Occupation: tailor, Nationality: Russian, Race: Hebrew, Last Residence: Noran, Destination: Boston, In Possession of: $10. But there, under Relatives, is the name: Cousin Kalman Fishtine, of 30 Parmenter Street, Boston, who is married to Max's first cousin Esther. That sealed it for me. Max has been found.

Furthermore, under Max's name is Benjalovitz, Chaye, 15, tailoress, and travelling as Max's sister, who is really Esther's sister.

Still curious about the name, I joined the Jewish Genealogical Society, which connected me to LitvakSIG, which is the Lithuanian source, using the District of Trakai, which included Aran.

I then went on a very amazing circuitous route, which not only gave me Max's family name, but also revealed what surely happened to what was left of his family during World War II.

From JGS I learned about a book titled "There Once Was A World, A 900 Year Chronicle of the Shtetl of Eishishok", by Yaffa Eliach. The name Eishishok (Eisiskes) was slightly familiar to me, and when I went to Max's diary, I found again that, in order to return to the United States, he and Chaye had to go to "Aysishok where I was registered and that was where my cousin was registered and we got our passports."

I got the Eliach book and found the passages that refer to Aran (Varena) and what happened to the Jewish villagers. The reports were that they were all killed in September 1941.

I wrote to Dr. Eliach to ask if there was anything else she could tell me about Aran. I got an answer from her husband who said she was very ill and could not answer.

An email appeared from Ranaan Isseroff, an associate of the Eliachs, asking if I had an answer to my letter to Dr. Eliach. I answered yes, but then she wanted to know my connection to Eishishok, so I told her about it and that I was hoping to find records of the passports.

She said that "Judy" would know about the passports.

I asked, "Who is Judy and how would I get in touch?"

Ranaan wrote to Judy.

Judy Baston, a member of JGS, wrote to me explaining that records of passports of that time were extremely hard to get, but not impossible. The records of Eishishok were kept in the JGS District of Lida. In the meantime, she would attach an Excel file.

The attachment was astonishing. It contained an Excel file in English of names and dates of the Beniatovich family, as it existed in 1904, going back to my great-great-great grandfather!

And there, on the list, was Mordkhei, son of Avram and grandson of Yosel Beniatovich amidst 44 of his relatives, confirming whatever background I had assembled. Since getting that file, we use the English spelling of Beniatovich.

Perhaps the official who signed the passports in Eiseskis or the official who made the Ivernia's manifest decided that the 'i' in Beniatovich was a 'j' and the 't' was an 'l' and wound up with Benjalovitz.

I am still amazed that a clerk in the immigration office had the curiosity and sense of duty to go through the manifest of the Ivernia to find Max's entry. If he had not done that, then Max might never have been approved for citizenship.

I have found more information on what happened to the Jews of Aran. The Jager Report is the most condemning.

We can all wonder how things would have turned out if Avram had returned to Palestine with his family and settled with Nathan.

BERNICE: Sid

Bernice wrote David a letter.

"When Alan was born, he was named for Max's father, whose name was Avram Aaron. I did not want an Abraham, so we called him Alan. For weeks after that Max refused to call him Alan. He referred to him as Avram. Eventually, he did call him Alan.

"When Joe was bedridden with MS, Max would drive to Quincy dressed in a suit, vest, tie, and a white shirt. He never veered, even on a ninety-degree day. He would stand at the door of Joe's bedroom, say hello, and then go directly to the dining room. He was unable to converse with Joe because it was so difficult for him. In the dining room, he would read the Sunday Times from cover to cover.

"When Sylvia died, he gave Ma, Dolly, and me strict orders not to show any hysterical crying, and we didn't.

"He was a bright man with his own beliefs. I remember he once said that God was Nature. I don't think he believed in a God, per se. After Ma died, he had nothing to do, so he went to synagogue with his cronies, but frankly, it was more social than his belief in prayer.

"One of his pleasures was to conduct Passover Seders, and, by golly, he did the whole service, cover to cover, and sat alone reading while the kids left the table after the meal.

"Well, anyone who went to Ford Hall Town meetings in those days was considered a socialist. He probably was. You know how he used to shout about politics.

"He was devastated when he lost Sylvia, when he lost Ma, and with Joe's illness. A lot of loss. Joe's death was the capper. The inscription on the family stone tells the story: *The inseparables in their life and in their death were not separated.*

"When the Malden Street Synagogue burned down, Max, as President, tried to raise money to rebuild. For months, only the foundation was done. The entire construction stopped for a year. It was known as Bennett's Folly. Eventually, it was rebuilt, but Max was not President then.

"He was quite a character, simple and complex, with a lot of emotional upheaval and turmoil internally."

DIAMONDS: David

I'll bet you a dollar Max never said, "I love you" to Lillian. That's not a criticism: probably very few of his generation ever said it. I think my generation was the one first trained by the women of my generation and by the movies to say the three magic words. And I want to thank them for it. I said "I love you" many times to my late wife Jane and I only wish I had said it a thousand times more than I did. Nowadays, with adult children, I never talk on the phone with any of them without saying "I love you" and they do too, unless talking from a business meeting.

I love that and I cherish it.

But certainly in all of history, men who couldn't get those words out found ways to convey their feelings.

Max did a good job with diamonds.

Besides the engagement ring, each time Lillian had a baby, Max gave her diamonds: in 1917 for Joseph, in 1920 for Irene Sylvia, in 1926 for me, and in 1930 for Sidney. In each case, except when I was born, it was a ring with a cluster of stones in complicated but handsome settings. The one my mother got when I was born was a single round stone, one-carat (something I found out much later), bigger than any stone in any of the other rings, in a basket setting. The clusters of diamonds in the other rings were serious stones, not chips by any means, and all those other rings were worth more than the one that was "mine." One, I think Sylvia's, had 12 stones, about a half carat each. These must not have been too hard for Max to buy when he had money before the Depression struck. He had been prospering like everyone else in the 20's, including acquiring real estate.

In fact, he owned three triple-deckers by the end of the '20's, including the one we lived in and the one the store was in, on Main Street in Everett. Somewhere in the late 20's, after the Crash hit, just as he had finished acquiring them, he had to unload them. Sid's recollection of the story is that he "walked away" from them. Mixed in with this, and probably a factor in having to give up these properties was Max's way of carrying people on credit who could not pay for their food or rent. They ran up tabs and Max couldn't bring himself to cut them off. All of this drove Lilly nuts, of course, and helped precipitate the move from the Main Street store to the Norwood Street store, where he broke the charge account habit. But there was still most of the Depression to go through and Max never really made much money until World War II, which helped his economy and everyone else's. So, guess what? During the '30's, I think three times, Max and Lillian went into Boston and got loans against the diamonds somewhere, or to put it less politely, they pawned them. To put it even less politely, the way we children referred to it, they hocked them. Maybe business bills were piling up, maybe tuition money was needed (Joey was in Harvard from 1934 to 1938), and maybe mortgage payments were needed. They had finally bought a house in 1937, or more precisely, Max had bought a house on Baker Road, the only single family house we ever lived in.

But what happened the last time they went to hock the diamonds?

In those days, there were men, maybe desperate to make a buck during the Depression, who roamed around cities with small cameras, and they would take your picture right there on the street. Then they would ask you for fifty cents, and write down your name and address. Maybe you wondered if you would ever get the photo.

But what if you had just been to hock the diamonds again, and you were upset, hurt and steaming, as was Lilly, and Max, who always walked a pace or two in front of everyone, was ahead of her on the sidewalk, carrying his hat and jacket on a hot day, looking beaten and disconsolate? If that happened to you, and a guy with a camera came up to you and said he had taken your picture, would you give him the money?

Well, they did.

And we have the picture to prove it.

In fact, the exotic double photo is why we know the story because we would ask, "What's this?" and receive this family legend for a reply. He always managed to get the rings out of hock. And what a relief that must have been each time.

In 1963, Lillian died at the age of 67. Some time after her death, Max gave all her rings to Joey and Bernice and eventually each of their sons Alan and Paul was given a ring for his future bride. Meanwhile, Joey and Bernice had "my" diamond made into a man's ring for Max.

On April 14, 1974, visiting my Auntie Dolly on Long Island for the Jewish Holidays, Max died, sitting upright in a wooden chair. Dolly called us in New Jersey and Jane and I jumped into the station wagon for the hour drive to Dolly's. Max was still sitting in the chair when we got there.

Dolly, who said to me she didn't trust the cops, handed me the ring, a wallet, a watch, some money, all of which she had removed from Max.

The funeral parlor in Malden, which had handled Lilly's funeral was notified and they arranged for the body to be shipped by American Airlines.

In what always seemed to me to be a final act of mischief on Max's part, he disappeared. American

Airlines couldn't find him. The pressure on everyone was tremendous, because Jews bury their dead the day after the death. Finally, American Airlines, which had screwed up royally, found Max and delivered him barely in time for the funeral service.

I noticed that the funeral service for Max was very sedate and there was no keening or wailing, as there was for Lilly's funeral in exactly the same place, with many of the same people, most of whom I didn't know.

I asked Max's lawyer, Morris Fulman, who had taken care of the arrangements, why it was so quiet. He explained to me that at 82, Max had lived the Biblical three score and ten and then some, so there was the sense in the Jewish culture that this didn't constitute a tragedy. At 67, Lilly had been cheated of her three score and ten, so that was the cause of the intensified mourning.

A couple of weeks later, Fulman had Sid and me in to read Max's will to us.

Max had several charities and institutions listed and after those were paid out, Sid and I would receive about $4,000 each. This was not an estate that was going to hit the front page of the New York Times, no matter what the Woodlawn Street house sold for. Fulman handled that, too. He was a lodge brother of Max's and was indispensable to Sid and me. I was in New Jersey and Sid was on Cape Cod, so we could never have done it without him. The house sold for $24,000 and covered Max's bequests.

By then I had had the ring appraised at Macy's in Manhattan, and when the will was settled, I gave Sid half the value.

A couple months later, an advertisement in the Record, the local New Jersey paper, announced that a jeweler was offering to reset stones in new settings at Bamberger's in the Garden State Mall and that reminded me why I had appropriated Max's ring in the first place. I had never given Jane a real engagement ring, and she was intrigued with the idea of changing the ring for her. We went out into the snowy, slushy night, which worked for us, because we were the only ones at the jewelry department where they were working on the rings. Jane picked a Tiffany setting and they put the diamond into it very quickly, right in front of us.

A happy ending, for the moment.

But the story wasn't quite over.

Jane died in 1987 at the age of 58. A few years later, when Michael announced engagement to his Laura, I gave him his mother's ring for her. It fit her hand with no alteration necessary.

DAVID: Sid

After the Circle Market, David moved to New York, found work with United Press as a caption writer, met and married Jane Harris, graduate of the famous Carnegie Tech Drama School, and had three children: Michael, Kathryn, and Laura.

David eventually worked for a few of the biggest advertising agencies in New York City: Grey; Dancer Fitzgerald Sampler; and McCaffery McCall as a copywriter. My favorite commercial that he wrote is the Santa Claus riding downhill on a Norelco shaver while the announcer says, "Christmas is a time for closeness."

After Jane died, he moved into the city, and became a victim of age downsizing. Then came Chatham, Cape Cod, next to my town of Harwich. He loved Cape Cod and utilized his photography experience to pay the bills.

He became ill with kidney problems. His daughter Kathryn found him an apartment in Boston before he needed dialysis treatments.

David died June 3, 2005 at Brigham and Women's Hospital. I visited a few days before. He was his usual alert, sarcastic self, giving nurses a hard time.

That's what I will remember. I learned my sarcasm from him. I learned punning from him. My brand of humor must come from him as well. I loved our word duels. I miss him.

End:

This was found in all the loose papers.

David wrote:

I think this should end –

On Oct 10, 1999, I saw on TV Chaz Palmiateri's *A Bronx Tale.*

Son says to DeNiro, "Dad, I'm sorry if I ever hurt you."

I cried uncontrollably for a few minutes, amazed at my reaction. Well, of course, I wish I had said that to Max.

www.ingramcontent.com/pod-product-compliance
Lightning Source LLC
Chambersburg PA
CBHW021125020426
42331CB00005B/629
* 9 7 8 0 9 8 2 2 6 6 3 1 1 *